W9-BMN-698

Munchies

**Cream Cheese
Hot Poppers**

**Baked Bird
with Goldfish Crust**

**Eggo Ice-Cream
Sandwiches**

Munchies

Cook what you want,
eat what you like.
Finally, a cookbook
even you will use.

by Kevin Telles Roberts

Storey Publishing

The mission of Storey Publishing is to serve our customers
by publishing practical information that encourages
personal independence in harmony with the environment.

Edited by Siobhan Dunn
Designed by Wendy Palitz
Cover photograph by Hugh Hartshorne
Interior photographs by Kevin Kennefick
Styled by Wendy Scofield
Cover styled by Mary Placek
Illustrations by Joel Holland
Text production by Jennifer Jepson Smith
Indexed by Jan Williams

Copyright © 2004 by Kevin Telles Roberts

All rights reserved. No part of this book may be reproduced without
written permission from the publisher, except by a reviewer who may
quote brief passages or reproduce illustrations in a review with
appropriate credits; nor may any part of this book be reproduced,
stored in a retrieval system, or transmitted in any form or by any means
— electronic, mechanical, photocopying, recording, or other —
without written permission from the publisher.

The information in this book is true and complete to the best of our
knowledge. All recommendations are made without guarantee on
the part of the author or Storey Publishing. The author and publisher
disclaim any liability in connection with the use of this information.
For additional information please contact Storey Publishing,
210 MASS MoCA Way, North Adams, MA 01247.

Storey books are available for special premium and promotional
uses and for customized editions. For further information, please call
1-800-793-9396.

Printed in the United States by Edwards Brothers
10 9 8 7 6 5 4 3 2

Library of Congress Cataloging-in-Publication Data

Roberts, Kevin T.
  Munchies : cook what you want, eat what you like / Kevin T. Roberts.
      p. cm.
  Includes index.
  ISBN-13: 978-1-58017-536-4 (pbk. : acid-free paper)
  ISBN-10: 1-58017-536-8 (pbk. : acid-free paper)
  1. Cookery. I. Title.
TX714 .R565 2004
641.5—dc22
                                          2003021729

To my mom, Ella Jayne Roberts. Without her spiritual, emotional, and loving support through the years, none of this would have been possible. I thank and love you, Mom.

Special Thanks

To my awesome nanny, Opal Fern Roberts. I value your wisdom and your crazy sense of humor. Thanks for supporting my creativity.

To Aunt Janice, Uncle Dave, Uncle Rich, and Stu. Thanks for your support.

To the rest of my extended family including Eric, Robyn, Emily, Charlie, and Emily. Thanks for your kindness and support.

Deborah Obad, Norman Kolpas, Siobhan Dunn, Pam Art, Janet Harris, Deborah Balmuth, Wendy Palitz, and Dianne Cutillo: Thanks for guiding and believing in me.

Thanks

To the rest of my family and friends, thanks for your friendship and recipes: Mike "Summertime" Simko, Cal Evans, Eric Hunter, the Campbells, the Livelys, Marc and Tina Merrie, Fernando Zuleta, Kent Buchanan, Jason Chauncey, Adam Cole, Bonz, Meeno, Dylan, and all the rest of you rats I've known for too long.

To all of my classmates from Melrose Avenue School, Eagle Rock High School, Apple School (Los Feliz Hills School), Cal State Northridge, and UCLA. Thanks for inspiring my creativity and keeping me out of trouble.

Recipe Acknowledgments

Chilean Po' Boy: Maria De Los Angeles
The Best Taco Salad Ever: Jason Chauncey
German Potato Salad: Atlas Sausage, North Hollywood, CA
Zucchini Boats: Ella Roberts
Cal's Cheesy Cauliflower: Cal Evans
Atomic Wings: Mike Simko
Super Tuna Melt: Eric Smith
Frozen Bananas & Chocolate: Michelle Moffett
Baked Apples & Cinnamon and Nanny's Homemade
    Applesauce: Opal Roberts
Mexican Tuna Wrap: Mark Livedale (R.I.P.)

Pistachio-Crusted Halibut: Inspired by
    The Cowboy Club, Sedona, AZ
Texas Caviar Bean Dip: Marc and Tina Merrie
    and Grandma Kloss
Dee's Best Salsa: Danielle Galvan
Bruschetta: Jenny Denouel
Coleslaw with Peanuts: Lawry's Tam O'Shanter Inn,
    Los Feliz, CA
Baked Beans with Pork: inspired by the man
    himself — Mr. Stubb
Breakfast Bagel Sandwich — thanks to all the Lexi-cons

Contents

Introduction

Welcome to the world of Munchies! Ever since I was a kid, I've had to fend for myself because I grew up in a single-parent home. My mom went to college and worked full time. My introduction to cooking came the day I turned on the oven and placed a Van de Kamp's frozen meal in it. About 20 minutes later, I opened the oven and my food was still frozen. The oven didn't appear hot, and I was wondering what that weird smell was. I grabbed a match and lit it right in front of the open oven door.

Kaboom!

That's right, I became a human fireball. I singed every hair on my body, which, thank God, wasn't much at the time. Talk about trial and error.

I started hounding Mom and Nanny (my grandma) to teach me the ways of the kitchen. As they explained them, I learned that cooking wasn't difficult at all. All I needed were some basic ingredients and an idea of what types of cooking utensils and which pot to use and I was on my way to Macaroni and Cheese Heaven — which, by the way, I ate every day for a month. After that got old, I started adding different stuff to it: hamburger, tuna, tomatoes, onions, and tons of ketchup. I knew I was on my way to Gourmet Macaroni and Cheese Heaven.

Another reason I started to cook for myself was that every time I saw a sign or commercial advertising some great meal deal that looked all big and juicy, I would order it. I'd be salivating while unwrapping it, but it always turned out small, dry, and wimpy. I was like, "Where is the meal deal I saw in the commercial?" Talk about a rip-off. Out of frustration, I went to the store, bought the exact same ingredients, and cooked one of those meals myself. I discovered I could make a better, bigger, and juicier product for less and even have leftovers for later or the next day. I knew I was on to something. Food Freedom!

There is a simpler and cheaper way to eat.

Cooking!

I wish that when I was in my teens, in school, or getting my first apartment there had been a cookbook or cooking show that satisfied my desire to learn to cook simple, cool, and original recipes. Finally I started creating and stashing away my own recipes as well as some created by my friends and family. Eventually I had hundreds of tasty recipes, so I created *Munchies*. I decided on the name *Munchies* because that's the term I use to describe just about anything that deals with food, drinks, and me being hungry — which seems to be all of the time.

Being born and stuck in Los Angeles helped shape my cooking. While growing up I had access to foods from different cultures all the time. One day I would have a hot dog, another day chicken teriyaki, and on the weekends I ate tacos. This opened up a whole world of food that I would never have discovered otherwise. You'll find a lot of my *Munchies* recipes reflect this eclectic style.

It's definitely cool to know how to cook. First of all, it automatically defines you as a independent person. Nobody likes someone who can't feed him- or herself. Second, the opposite sex finds it sexy. Cooking is very primal. Only the strong will survive. Let me tell you, the only way people survived back in the old days was by cooking! Just because you killed a big buffalo and dragged it 10 miles didn't make you the man. You had to know what to do with it; no one ate buffalo sushi. Someone had to cook it. And I guarantee whoever was doing the cooking was getting all the love. You have to go through the stomach to get to the heart.

I have fused my love of writing and love of food to create this comfort cookbook. Although these recipes are simple and easy, you still need to know the basics, like how to make a sandwich, boil water, and scramble eggs. If you don't, I suggest you move back in with your parents and start collecting government checks.

The recipes in this book are ideal because you can make them at any time of the day and for whatever mood you are in. They reflect the creative juices and independence that dwell within all young people out on their own for the first time. So, let's break this down: Cooking your own food saves money, is an impressive skill in the dating world, puts you on equal footing with at least the cavemen, and lets you have exactly what you want all the time. Freedom, independence, creativity — that's what *Munchies* is all about.

If you have any questions, comments, or recipes to share, or if you just want to say "Blah, blah, blah," you can e-mail me at **munchiescookbook@yahoo.com.**

Kevin T. Roberts

The Basics

This is required reading for all who are still learning their way around the kitchen and haven't stocked the pantry. You need to be familiar with common kitchen equipment before you start cooking. And if you're planning to use more than a few of these recipes, it makes sense for you to buy some ingredients — the ones that will keep on the shelf — ahead of time. These are the basic necessities for your cooking success.

❋ **Saucepans.** You'll need a small one and a large one.

❋ **Heavy ovenproof skillet.** *Ovenproof* just means that it should be all metal (usually iron or ceramic-coated iron) instead of plastic or wood so you can start on the stove and move into the oven with the same pan.

❋ **Small sauté pan.** For frying an egg, or heating up a sauce for one.

❋ **Roasting pan.** This is good for oven cooking — roasting meat, a whole chicken, or veggies.

❋ **Baking dish.** Get at least one of these, preferably two.

❋ **Baking sheet.** A baking sheet is good to have for all kinds of stuff, especially for cooking meats because it catches the drippings.

❋ **Big pot.** For boiling lots of stuff — spaghetti, for one.

❋ **Set of mixing bowls.** Get at least two microwave-safe bowls — large and small — if not a whole set.

✻ Strainer or colander. Mandatory for draining pastas and veggies.

✻ Toaster oven. Believe me, this is an essential.

✻ Measuring cups. Splurge on a complete set.

✻ Measuring spoons. Ditto — 1 tablespoon of hot chili powder is NOT the same as ½ teaspoon. You will regret the difference.

✻ Knives: Get one good knife. *You will cook better with a sharp knife!*

✻ Can opener: Duh.

If You Live to Cook Again

Stuff you'll want if you cook more than three times a year.

✻ Cooling rack

✻ Double boiler

✻ Liquid measure

✻ Whisk

✻ Spatula

✻ Grater

✻ Cutting board

✻ Assorted wooden spoons

✻ Rolling pin

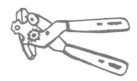

✻ Vegetable peeler

✻ Pot holders and a heavy-duty oven mitt

✻ Aluminum foil

✻ Resealable heavy-duty freezer bags

✻ Assortment of reusable plastic storage containers

✻ Plastic clothespins

Essential Munchie Freezer Items

* A bag of frozen chicken wings

* Tortillas — they keep really well in the freezer

* English Muffins

* Bagels — slice them before freezing and they're easy to reheat

* Pizza crust or frozen pizza

* Frozen burritos or pot pies

* Cookie dough

* Cool Whip

* Eggos or other frozen waffle

* Frozen fruit — great for making quick shakes or adding to ice cream, frozen berries are particularly useful.

* Frozen mixed vegetables — worth having if you don't have access to fresh veggies all the time, they are so much better than anything out of a can.

* Ore Ida Tater Tots

* Sausage — most sausages keep well in the freezer.

* Ground beef or turkey — pre-formed patties are easiest.

* Butter — it freezes and never goes bad!

* Coffee — keeping it in the freezer keeps it from becoming stale and losing flavor.

Chapter 1

Eye-Openers

Get out of bed—you've got a whole 24 hours to fill with Munchies.
Breakfast is the most important meal of the day. It rouses your metabolism, which kick-starts the fat-burning process. Enjoy these delicious recipes for all your fat-burning needs as well as a few for those high-calorie lazy Sundays. If you are not a die-hard breakfast eater and like to keep hitting the snooze button in the morning, make something the night before and bring it to work or class.

Breakfast Burrito

I used to work as a production coordinator on commercials and had to get up before dawn — I lived on these. The more ingredients, the bigger the tortilla you'll need.

Ingredients

½ teaspoon olive oil

2–3 mushrooms, chopped

1 thick onion slice, minced

½ tomato, chopped

2–3 spinach leaves, chopped

1 breakfast sausage, chopped

½ cup ground beef or chopped steak

2 or 3 large eggs

1 large flour tortilla

¼ avocado, chopped

2 tablespoons shredded cheese of your choice

Hot sauce
(my favorite with this recipe is Cholula)

The Steps

1. Heat the olive oil in a large skillet over high heat.

2. Sauté the mushrooms, onion, tomato, spinach leaves, sausage, and beef for 5 minutes, until the meat starts to brown.

3. With a fork, beat the eggs in a cup until smooth.

4. Pour the eggs into the skillet and scramble with the meat and vegetables, stirring occasionally.

5. Heat the tortilla by laying it directly over the skillet with the eggs in it or in a toaster oven, until it is warm but not toasted, about 1 minute.

6. Pour the skillet ingredients into the center of the tortilla. Sprinkle with the avocado and cheese.

7. Add the hot sauce to taste, then fold and roll the tortilla, tucking in the sides so you don't lose anything. Stuff in your mouth and eat.

Serves 1

Eye-Opening Hot Sauces

It is my opinion that hot sauce is the perfect condiment at every meal and on almost every food; breakfast is no exception. Try some of these on your eggs and I guarantee you won't be trying to crawl back into bed. For more info on hot sauce, check out the Cool Products guide at the end of this book (page 180).

* **Cholula Hot Sauce:** a standard red Mexican pepper sauce, good on practically everything.

* **Crystal:** Louisiana hot sauce made with cayenne pepper, mild enough for breakfast.

* **Frank's Original Red Hot:** a great basic hot sauce, as good on potatoes as it is on wings.

* **Louisiana Hot Sauce:** not too hot but enough to wake up your eggs.

* **Marie Sharp's Mild Habanero Pepper Sauce:** a perfect hot sauce with lime and carrots for mildness, made in the mountains of Belize. It's worth hunting down.

* **Picka Peppa Sauce, Original and Red Hot:** the classic Jamaican hot sauce, a little sweet and delicious on everything.

* **Tabasco:** a chipotle pepper sauce, but try the habanero one for extra kick.

Tater-Tot Hash

I grew up on Ore-Ida Tater Tots. I like to dunk them in my runny eggs. Here's a hearty breakfast you will love. And you can top it with your own runny eggs if you wish.

Ingredients

2 tablespoons olive or vegetable oil

1 green pepper, finely chopped

1 medium white onion, finely chopped

2 slices of ham or sausage, diced into ½ inch pieces

20 defrosted Tater Tots

Salt and freshly ground black pepper

The Steps

1. Preheat the oven to 450°F.

2. Heat the oil in a large ovenproof skillet over medium heat.

3. Sauté the green pepper, onion, and ham until the onion is translucent and the green pepper is tender, about 2 minutes.

4. Add the Tater Tots and sauté for another 3 to 4 minutes, turning occasionally until the Tots are crispy and hot.

5. Place the skillet in the oven. Bake for 10 to 15 minutes, until the Tater Tots are golden brown and crispy. Salt and pepper to taste.

Serves 2

Corned Beef Hash & Eggs

Hash is so good, I eat it every Saturday. Great with eggs any style.

Ingredients

½ teaspoon olive oil

½ small green pepper, chopped

½ medium-sized onion, chopped

1 teaspoon hot sauce of your choice
(see Eye-Opening Hot Sauces, page 9)

1 clove garlic, minced

Salt and freshly ground black pepper

1 can (16 ounces) corned beef hash

½ cup shredded Cheddar

2 large eggs, soft-boiled, poached, or fried

The Steps

1. Heat the oil in a heavy skillet over medium heat.

2. Increase the heat to high and sauté the pepper, onion, hot sauce, garlic, and salt and pepper to taste until the onion starts to soften, about 1 minute.

3. Add the hash, reduce the heat to medium, and cook for 5 to 10 minutes, stirring frequently, until brown and crispy.

4. Sprinkle the cheese evenly over the hash, cover, and cook another 2 minutes, or until the cheese is melted.

5. Top with the eggs.

Serves 1

Egg Safety

Eggs are organic products that require attention in terms of storing, handling, and cooking. The most important thing is never to eat raw or partially cooked eggs. Make sure your eggs are properly refrigerated and clean and uncracked before cooking. Always keep your cooking surfaces clean and wash your hands and utensils with hot water and soap.

Waffle Heaven

When you are on the move, in a rush, or, like me, perpetually late, this very simple and quick breakfast can be prepared three ways, depending on how late you are running.

The Steps

Ingredients

OPTION 1

2 teaspoons cream cheese

2 frozen waffles, toasted

1 teaspoon jelly

OPTION 1: You are just a little late.

1. Spread the cream cheese evenly on both waffles.

2. Spread the jelly evenly on top of the cream cheese.

3. Assemble as a sandwich or eat separately, like toast.

OPTION 2

2 teaspoons peanut butter

2 frozen waffles, toasted

1 banana, sliced

¼ teaspoon honey

OPTION 2: You are late, too late to stop for coffee. You will be drinking it from a vending machine, so you might as well slow down and make something for yourself to eat.

1. Spread the peanut butter evenly on both waffles.

2. Arrange the banana on top of the peanut butter.

3. Drizzle the honey on top.

OPTION 1
Late

OPTION 2
Later

OPTION 3
Hopeless

Ingredients

OPTION 3

2 teaspoons
cream cheese

2 frozen waffles,
toasted

1 large egg,
fried or scrambled

The Steps

OPTION 3: You are so late now it doesn't matter.
No one will believe your pathetic excuses anyway.
Have breakfast — you won't regret it!

1. Spread the cream cheese evenly on both waffles.

2. Pile the cooked egg on top of the cream cheese.

3. Assemble as a sandwich and run out the door. Or take
a more leisurely approach — make some coffee and use
a knife and fork.

Serves 1

Drowned Potatoes

Here is another variation on eggs and potatoes. I prefer russet, but white or red potatoes will work fine too.

Ingredients

2 small potatoes

2 large eggs

1 teaspoon olive oil or butter

Salt and freshly ground black pepper

Ketchup or salsa, if desired

The Steps

1. Clean and cut the potatoes into ¼-inch pieces. They need to be small so they will cook quickly.

2. Crack the eggs into a bowl and beat until smooth.

3. Heat the oil in a medium-sized skillet over high heat. Tilt to coat the entire pan and reduce the heat to medium. Do not let the oil burn or smoke.

4. Dunk the cut potatoes in egg and ladle just the potatoes into the skillet. Cook for 5 to 10 minutes, or until the potatoes are just tender, stirring often.

5. Pour the remaining eggs into the skillet and continue to cook until the eggs are no longer runny and the potatoes are nice and tender.

6. Season with salt and pepper to taste. Top with ketchup or salsa, if desired.

Serves 2

The Italian Egg & Muffin Sandwich

This homemade version won't create a gut bomb like its greasy fast-food counterpart. I'm going to let you in on a little secret — ground cumin and egg go together perfectly.

Ingredients

1 teaspoon olive oil

2 cloves garlic, minced

¼ teaspoon dried oregano

2 large eggs

2 English muffins, halved

2 tablespoons Parmesan

Secret Ingredient

½ teaspoon ground cumin

The Steps

1. Heat the oil in a small skillet over medium heat.

2. Sauté the garlic and oregano for 2 to 3 minutes, until the garlic starts to brown slightly. Be careful not to let it burn once it begins to brown.

3. Crack the eggs directly into the skillet and scramble with a fork. Cook 2 to 5 minutes, until it is set, creamy, and moist.

4. Meanwhile, toast the English muffins.

5. Mix the Parmesan and cumin into the scrambled eggs.

6. Pile the eggs on the bottom halves of the English muffins. Top and eat.

Serves 2

Hawaiian Roman Toast

The Romans actually invented French toast. My twist on this classic recipe is to use King's Hawaiian bread. It's a thick, fluffy egg bread that's perfect for French toast. If you can't find it, any sweet egg bread will work, like Portuguese sweet bread or challah.
If you have it, this is the time to break out the real maple syrup. Otherwise, Aunt Jemima works.

Ingredients

2 large eggs, beaten

1 tablespoon cinnamon

4 slices Kings Hawaiian bread, 1–2 inches thick and cut in half diagonally

4 tablespoons butter, ½ tablespoon per slice plus 2 tablespoons for the pan

½ cup pure maple syrup, warmed

Secret Ingredient

1 tablespoon vanilla

The Steps

1. Mix the eggs, cinnamon, and vanilla in a large bowl.

2. Dunk bread into the egg mixture to coat thoroughly. You can let it sit in the egg in order to soak it up.

3. Melt 2 tablespoons of the butter in a large skillet over medium-high heat.

4. Cook the slices of eggy bread in the butter until golden brown, 3 to 5 minutes on each side.

5. Serve with butter and the warmed maple syrup.

Serves 2

Cottage Cheese with Fruit & Honey

The name says it all. Cottage cheese is actually full of protein. You can use any kind of fruit, but peaches are the tastiest. This is an easy breakfast to take with you or even make at work or school.

The Steps

1. Mix the cottage cheese, the peaches, and the honey in a bowl.

2. Divide evenly into two serving bowls.

3. Eat immediately or chill.

2 servings

Ingredients

2 cups cottage cheese

2 peaches, chopped

2 teaspoons honey

Frying an egg is one of the most enjoyable cooking methods I know. But it's like a summer blockbuster: Eventually you're ready for something a little more subtle. **Experiment with your breakfast eggs before you get too old and set in your ways.**

Fried

Melt butter or oil in a skillet over medium-high heat. You can use as much as you like but any less than a tablespoon and you will have an unsuccessful fried egg experience. Crack the egg on the edge of the pan. If you are cool, you can do this with one hand. Let the egg free-fall into pan. Sizzle until the white is cooked enough to slide your spatula under it. Now here is your big decision, to flip or not to flip. If you really like a runny egg, don't turn it over. Let the whites get a little brown on the edges and completely cooked. If you are squeamish about runny eggs, then flip the egg gently so as not to break the yolk, let it cook for another 30 seconds or so, and remove. If you want your egg to resemble roadkill, break the yolk by pressing on the egg with the spatula. You can work out any remaining aggression by crushing the empty shell in your fist.

Soft-Boiled

Gently lower the egg, in its shell, into softly boiling water. Let it cook for 3 to 4 minutes, then remove. Run the egg under cold tap water for about 30 seconds. Gently crack the egg by tapping it with a spoon or against the counter. Peel off the top of the shell so you can get a spoon in and scoop out the egg. Serve on top of toast, potatoes, or hash. You can also eat a soft-boiled egg right from the shell — that's what those funny egg cups your grandmother has are for. Just remove the top part of the shell and use a teaspoon to spoon the egg out directly into your mouth, or use a strip of toast and dip it in.

Poached

This is the trickiest of all egg cooking methods. Boil water in a saucepan, then reduce the heat so it is simmering. Add 1 tablespoon of white vinegar to the water. Very gently crack the egg and carefully open it so it falls directly into the hot water. Some of the white will disperse and foam but the majority should immediately firm up around the yolk and turn bright white. You should have a little bundle of egg whites bobbing in the not quite boiling water. The whites are essentially cooked at this point, so you just have to decide how runny you like the yolks. Three minutes is cooked; cook for longer for a harder yolk. Remove the egg from the water with a spoon and drain it. Serve on top of toast, bacon, or hash.

Rosemary Roasted Red Potatoes

*You can use russet potatoes, but while testing this recipe,
I realized small red potatoes are better. Before cooking, scrub
the potatoes well under cold water. Roasted potatoes are always
good for breakfast and are delicious with eggs any style.
These are great with ketchup and/or hot sauce.*

Ingredients

2 tablespoons
olive oil

1 fistful
(about 5 sprigs)
fresh rosemary

5 cloves garlic,
chopped

10 small red
potatoes, cut into
quarters

Salt and freshly
ground black
pepper

The Steps

1. Preheat oven to 450°F. Lightly grease a shallow metal baking dish that is big enough to hold all the potatoes. An 8-inch or 2-quart dish will work.

2. Heat the oil in a large skillet over high heat.

3. Sauté the rosemary and garlic for about 2 minutes, until they smell strong but are not yet browning.

4. Add the potatoes and salt and pepper to taste; mix well to coat. Reduce the heat to medium-high and cook for 5 minutes, until potatoes are hot and well coated with the seasonings.

5. Transfer the potatoes to the baking dish and bake for 15 minutes. Remove the dish from the oven, toss the potatoes to make sure they are browning evenly and not sticking, then bake for another 15 minutes, until potatoes are completely cooked and tender when poked with a fork.

6. Turn the oven to broil and stick the baking dish under the broiler for 3 to 5 minutes, until the potatoes are completely browned and crispy. (This is the trick to making them really crunchy.)

Serves 2 or 3

Parboil

A little trick to make your potatoes cook faster is to partially cook them in boiling water before baking or frying. This is an especially clever trick if you have a microwave. Just wash and cut up the potatoes as directed in your recipe and microwave them for a minute or more, until they just barely start to cook and become tender. At this point you can easily fry them up or add them to soups and baked dishes, or you can run them under cold water to stop the cooking and set them aside until needed.

Breakfast Bagel Sandwich

I used to eat these for breakfast when I was a manager at a corporation. Nothing is scarier than having to get up and go to work when it's still dark out. On top of that I had to wear a suit.

Ingredients

1 bagel, sliced

2 tablespoons cream cheese

1 slice onion

1 slice tomato

2 slices turkey or ham

The Steps

1. Toast the bagel (if you have time).

2. Spread the cream cheese evenly on both bagel halves.

3. Pile the onion, tomato, and turkey on the bottom half.

4. Top the sandwich and cut in half.

Serves 1

Chapter 2

Sammies

This is the nickname I gave sandwiches when I was a kid. Sadly, I still refer to them this way. My friends give me weird looks every time I do, which happens many times a day because sandwiches are great all the time, at every meal — breakfast, lunch, dinner, even late-night snacks. (See my Eggo Ice-Cream Sandwiches as a case in point.) Even if you claim never to have cooked anything, you've probably made a sandwich. So read on and be inspired by some of these classic, and not so classic, variations on *something* between two slices of bread.

Egg Salad Sandwich

I use ranch dressing instead of mayonnaise to give this recipe a bolder taste. I also use cayenne pepper instead of regular pepper so it has a nice bite.

Ingredients

2 hard-cooked eggs, chopped

1 tablespoon ranch dressing

¼ teaspoon cayenne pepper

Salt

2 slices bread, toasted, if desired

(whatever you have —
pumpernickel is
good, but so is thin
white bread)

2 slices tomato

The Steps

1. In a small bowl, mix the eggs, dressing, cayenne, and salt to taste.

2. Spread the egg salad evenly on one slice of the bread, then top with the tomatoes and the second slice to make the sandwich.

Makes 1 sandwich

Fried Bologna Sandwich

Need I say more? To keep the bologna flat while cooking, hold it down with your spatula.

Ingredients

4 slices bologna

2 teaspoons mayonnaise*

2 slices bread, toasted, if desired
(whatever you have — of course Wonder Bread would be the classic accompaniment here)

2 slices tomato

The Steps

1. Cook the bologna slices in a skillet over medium heat until they get a little charred around the edges and start to curl. Lay the bologna slices on paper towels to absorb the excess fat. Drain any excess fat from the pan. (Okay, let's be real: Draining the fat will never make this a low-fat treat, but for some reason it makes me feel better.)

2. Spread the mayo on both slices of the bread.

3. Add tomato slices to one slice of bread, top with the bologna, and make it a sandwich with the other slice of bread.

Makes 1 sandwich

✳ Use a spicy mustard instead of mayo.

Fried Egg & Cream Cheese Sandwich

I like my eggs over-medium with the yolks still runny. *

Ingredients

1 tablespoon
butter or oil

2 large eggs

1 tablespoon
cream cheese

2 slices bread,
toasted

Salt and freshly
ground black pepper

Hot sauce or
mustard, if desired

The Steps

1. Melt the butter in a medium-sized skillet over medium-high heat.

2. Fry the eggs until the whites are set and the yolks reach the desired runniness.

3. Spread the cream cheese on both slices of the toast.

4. Place the eggs on one slice of toast, season with the salt and pepper to taste and the hot sauce (if desired), and make it a sandwich with the other slice.

Makes 1 sandwich

✳ See Egg Safety about runny eggs, page 11.

Italian Chicken Sandwich

Definitely put the cheese on the bread and then toast it so it's nice and melted. It doesn't hurt to add Parmesan to this sandwich.

Ingredients

1 large egg, beaten

¼ cup Italian
bread crumbs

2 boneless chicken
breasts, skinned

2 tablespoons
tomato sauce

2 Italian or French
rolls, cut in half
lengthwise

2 slices
Monterey Jack

The Steps

1. Preheat the oven to 450°F.

2. Beat the egg in a small bowl.

3. Put the bread crumbs in a separate bowl or plate with a high lip.

4. Drench each chicken breast in egg, then coat with the bread crumbs.

5. Place the coated chicken breasts in a small baking dish and bake for 30 to 40 minutes, or until the chicken is white in the center.

6. Spread the tomato sauce on the rolls and add the cheese. Heat for a few minutes in the oven or toaster oven so the cheese starts to melt.

7. Add the breaded chicken to the rolls and make sandwiches. Another way of toasting the cheese is to lay the cheese slices directly on the chicken breasts for the last minute or so of baking.

Makes 2 sandwiches

Pita Melts

You have two options with these sammies. You can go egg salad and Monterey Jack or tuna salad and Cheddar.

The Steps

1. Preheat the oven or toaster oven to 375°F.

2. Mix the eggs with the mayo in a bowl.

3. Slice along one edge of each pita to open the pockets.

4. Stuff half of the egg salad and two slices of the cheese into each pita.

5. Toast the stuffed pitas for 6 to 10 minutes, or until the pitas are browned and the cheese is melted.

Makes 2 sandwiches

Ingredients

4 large hard-cooked eggs, chopped
or
1 can tuna, drained and chopped

2 tablespoons mayonnaise

4 slices Monterey Jack or Cheddar

2 pita breads

The Pita Options

As ever, fresh tomato, onion, or lettuce will improve almost any sandwich. Watercress and arugula are gourmet options that taste great on egg salad. Make your pita sandwich with chicken salad if you are tired of egg and tuna. If you cut the pita in half, you can create two sandwich flavors. Try any of the following additions; they all go great with egg or tuna salad:

* Chopped sweet pickles

* Capers

* Chopped marinated peppers

* Green olives

* 1 tablespoon Dijon mustard

* 1 teaspoon curry powder, paprika, or cayenne

* 1 teaspoon celery salt or 1 stalk of diced celery (for some crunch)

* Fresh or dried dill

* Fresh parsley

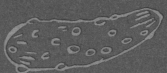

Sourdough Melt

This recipe works best with a sourdough baguette or any type of long French baguette.

Ingredients

2 tablespoons mustard

6–10 slices roasted turkey

6–10 slices salami

5 slices Pepper Jack

1 tomato, thinly sliced

1 sourdough baguette, cut in half lengthwise

Salt and freshly ground black pepper

The Steps

1. Preheat the oven or toaster oven to 375°F.

2. Arrange the mustard, turkey, salami, cheese, and tomato on the baguette. Season with the salt and pepper to taste.

3. Bake open faced for 5 to 10 minutes, or until the bread is toasted and the cheese is melted. Put the sandwich together, divide in half, and enjoy.

Makes 2 sandwiches

The BLAT

This is the almost classic version of a BLT except I add avocado and a spicy chipotle-mayo sauce. It makes all the difference.

Ingredients

5 slices bacon

1 tablespoon mayonnaise

1 chipotle pepper, seeded and minced

¼ teaspoon cayenne pepper

Salt and freshly ground black pepper

2 slices toasted sourdough, rye, or whole wheat bread

1 lettuce leaf, big enough to fit the size of the bread

¼ avocado, sliced

2 slices tomato

The Steps

1. Cook the bacon in a small skillet until crispy, about 7 minutes. Drain on paper towels.

2. Mix the mayo, chipotle pepper, cayenne, and salt and pepper to taste in a small bowl.

3. Spread the spicy mayo on each slice of the toast.

4. Add the bacon, lettuce, avocado, and tomatoes to one slice, building the layers to make the best BLAT you have ever had. Top with the remaining piece of toast and dig in.

Makes 1 sandwich

Beverly Hills Burger

A burger is a burger, I know. But try some of these interesting options before you cook, and it's now an artsy, frou-frou burger. Remember, you want to make the patty a little bigger than the bun because the meat shrinks when it's cooked. You don't want to end up with a meatball on the grill and everyone laughing at you.

The Steps

1. Shape the beef into four round patties each slightly larger than a hamburger bun.

2. Season with the ingredients of your choice.

3. Grill on the barbecue or fry in a skillet until cooked through unless you like them bloody. (See note about beef doneness on page 42.)

4. Place the burgers on the buns, top, and feast.

Serves 4

Ingredients

1 pound ground beef or turkey

Seasonings of choice
(see box on opposite page)

4 hamburger buns

The Burger Options

✱ Add 1 egg yolk, chopped parsley, and bread crumbs to the ground meat before forming patties.

✱ Add a splash of soy sauce, ground pepper to taste, and a tablespoon of garlic chili paste.

✱ Add a few drops of Worcestershire sauce and a small diced onion.

✱ For a curry burger, add 4 tablespoons of hot chutney (either tomato or mango), 1 tablespoon of curry powder, a small diced onion or 1 teaspoon of onion flakes, and 1 teaspoon of dried parsley.

✱ Mix capers and diced shallots into the meat along with a tablespoon of dried mustard powder.

I could go on but you get the idea — most of the condiments and toppings that you put *on* your burger can easily go *in* your burger. This is a great trick at cookouts, too.

The Chilean Po' Boy

My friend Maria De Los Angeles and I talk about food all day because the company we work for doesn't feed us. This po' boy is inspired by one she used to eat in Chile.

Ingredients

10 ounces roast beef, about 2 handfuls

2 cans (2–4 ounces each) French-cut green beans, cold

2 of your favorite crusty sandwich rolls, toasted

Hot sauce

(Sriracha or a green habanero sauce is best. See Hot Sauce List, page 47, for other options)

Salt and freshly ground black pepper

The Steps

1. Warm the roast beef in a skillet for a few minutes, until the meat is hot. If you don't have time for this, nuke it for less than a minute.

2. Open up the cans of green beans, rinse, and set aside.

3. Split the rolls down one side. You may need to pull out some of the bread from the center to make a little room.

4. Pile the warm roast beef into the rolls. Lay the beans on top of the roast beef. Season with the hot sauce and salt and pepper to taste.

Makes 2 sandwiches

Whatever You Call It

Po' boys, hoagies, grinders, subs, wedgies, heroes, torpedoes, you name it. They all say big sandwich to me **and that means I want to eat them**.

Po' boys are Cajun; you won't find a sub or grinder in New Orleans. The classic is fried oyster or catfish and the bread should be a crusty French loaf. Po' boys can be made with meat (usually roast beef) like a regular sub and they come dressed and undressed, which refers to whether or not you want lettuce, tomato, mayo, mustard, pickle, etc.

Heroes, grinders, and subs all fall into the Italian tradition — the bread is crusty and the meat is usually a type of salami or other cured meat. They can have cheese and other toppings too. Traditionally, these sandwiches are big and they never have mayo. Oil and vinegar or Italian dressing does the trick.

In Philadelphia you get a hoagie or a Philly Cheese Steak. A hoagie is often hot with sautéed peppers and onions, as is the classic cheese steak. A wedgie is basically a calzone for the uninitiated and a torpedo is a sub on a torpedo roll (yep, it's shaped like a torpedo).

Call it what you like; it will depend on what part of the country you were raised in. They all taste great and all you need to turn a regular sandwich into one is the right length of bread and some imagination. Don't try this at home with sliced sandwich bread — that would be a serious violation.

Filling: Any type of cured pork or beef — salami, prosciutto, spiced ham, parma ham. Or go for steak, roast beef, or turkey.

Extras: Start with cheese. The best are provolone, mozzarella, and any other easy melting cheese. Other extras are peppers, onions, basil, sliced tomato, chopped sweet pickle, and roasted or marinated peppers.

The dressings: A po' boy is all about the mayo; try flavored ones. A hero takes oil and vinegar. The trick is good bread and lots of contrasting flavors, so experiment and get used to measuring your sandwich in inches.

CHEESE

DELI MEATS

Messy Russian Turkey

This sammie is one I eat all the time. I didn't even think to put it in this book until my editor, Siobhan, said, "It has to go in, you knucklehead." So here it is. One note: The more stuff you put on this, the messier it's going to get, which is a good thing.

Ingredients

2 pieces bread, my fave is sourdough

3 tablespoons Russian dressing

2–5 slices turkey

½ avocado

The Steps

1. Toast your bread. Spread dressing on both pieces.

2. Place the turkey on one piece of the toast.

3. Mash the avocado in a small bowl, so it is still chunky but spreadable. Spread it on the other slice of bread.

4. Assemble and eat.

Makes 1 sandwich

Homemade Russian Dressing

1 tablespoon mayo
1 tablespoon relish
1 tablespoon ketchup

(add a little hot sauce to get this fired up)

Mix well.

(I like to make extra so I can dunk my sammie in the sauce)

Options

✳ Homemade Russian Dressing

✳ Bacon: Add 2 to 5 slices of fried bacon

✳ Tomato: Add 2 thin slices

✳ Cheese: 1 slice of Monterey Jack or Swiss

Chapter 3

Animal

All the recipes in this section come from an animal or have animal in them. I recommend eating it for the quality of the nutrients it contains, if not in quantity. Why eat burgers when you can eat steak! Meat is generally cheaper than you think and you can always look for deals or specials at the supermarket. For a couple of bucks, you can get a nice cut of meat and cook it the way *you* like it. Who knows what you are getting in a fast-food place, anyway? If you really miss those little packets of salt and ketchup, take some home with you.

Stuffed Green Peppers

You can use ground turkey or ground beef. Don't forget to keep the tops of the green peppers.

Ingredients

4 large green peppers

1 tablespoon olive oil

5 cloves garlic, chopped

1 small onion, chopped

1 pound ground turkey or beef

1 can (12-ounces) tomato sauce

½ teaspoon dried oregano

½ teaspoon dried rosemary

½ teaspoon dried thyme

Salt and freshly ground black pepper

½ cup Parmesan cheese

½ cup bread crumbs

The Steps

1. Preheat oven to 450°F. Line a baking sheet with aluminum foil.

2. Carefully cut off the pepper tops about 1 inch from the stem and set them aside. Remove seeds and membranes from the peppers.

3. Heat the olive oil in a large skillet over medium-high heat.

4. Cook the garlic, onion, turkey, tomato sauce, oregano, rosemary, thyme, and salt and pepper to taste for about 5 minutes, stirring often, until the mixture comes to a low boil.

5. Mix the Parmesan cheese and bread crumbs in a bowl.

6. Remove the skillet from the heat and mix the Parmesan and bread crumbs into the meat sauce.

7. Stuff each of the green peppers to the top with this filling. Replace the tops.

8. Bake on the prepared sheet for 30 minutes, or until the peppers are tender.

Serves 2

Tips

✳ If you don't have all the dried herbs, try using 1 teaspoon of a general Italian herb mix instead.

✳ You don't actually eat the pepper tops — they just look cool and sophisticated.

Pork con Queso Tacos

Don't invite over too many friends for these or you'll go hungry.

Ingredients

1 pound pork
tenderloin

Salt and freshly
ground black
pepper

1 tablespoon
vegetable oil

8 ounces (1 cup)
shredded
Monterey Jack

8 taco-sized soft
corn tortillas

1. Boil the pork in a pot with enough water to cover it for 20 to 30 minutes, or until cooked through. It's cooked when white all the way through. There should not be pink on the meat at all.

2. Cut tenderloin into 1-inch cubes. Season with the salt and pepper to taste and set aside in a medium bowl.

3. Heat the oil in a medium-sized skillet over medium heat.

4. Place a few cubes of pork and 2 ounces (1 tablespoon) of the cheese in a tortilla and fold in half. Lightly fry each side until the tortilla is brown and the cheese is melting. Repeat with each taco, adding more oil if necessary. You can eat each taco as it comes out of the skillet or set them on a plate or aluminum foil in the oven on low heat to keep them warm.

Serves 2, four tacos each – of course you can eat them all yourself . . .

The Taco Options

✳ Serve tacos with extra hot sauce, guacamole, sour cream, chopped tomato, onion, or pepper. Try different salsas and cheeses.

✳ Experiment with hot chiles, but be careful! There is nothing worse than a taco that you can't eat because you've made it too hot to swallow.

Baked Beans with Pork

This recipe was inspired by the one and only Mr. Stubb. Because, ladies and gentlemen, he is a cook. Polish sausage works well with this recipe.

Ingredients

2 pork sausages, cut into 1-inch slices, cooked or raw

1 can (28 ounces) baked beans

¼ cup brown sugar

1 small onion, chopped

1 jalepeño pepper, seeded and minced

⅓ cup Stubb's Bar-B-Q Sauce

Salt and freshly ground black pepper

8 slices bacon

The Steps

1. Preheat oven to 350°F. Lightly grease a large baking dish.

2. Mix the sausage, beans, brown sugar, onion, jalapeño pepper, barbecue sauce, and salt and pepper to taste in a large bowl.

3. Transfer the mixture to the baking dish. Lay the bacon strips on top in a single layer.

4. Bake, uncovered, for 50 to 60 minutes, until hot throughout and the bacon is sizzling and brown on top.

Serves 2

If It's Still Mooing, It's Not Done

To tell if your steak is cooked, cut the steak at its thickest point. If it's still pretty pink and bloody, you call it **rare**; if it is just a little pink, call it **medium**; if there is no pink and the steak has started to smoke, it is **well done**. If your steak is still blue and cold inside, you could wind up with mad cow disease or something — put it back in the oven or skillet and be more patient.

Of course, the actual cooking times will vary depending on the weight or thickness of the meat and how hot your grill is. The best thing is to test the meat and put it back if you have any doubts. Here is a loose guideline for a 1½-pound steak that is 1½ inches thick.

Bloody: 7 to 10 minutes (3 to 5 minutes on each side)

Less bloody: 12 to 16 minutes (6 to 8 minutes on each side)

Well-done to charred: 20 to 25 minutes (10+ minutes on each side) — any longer and you can use it for charcoal.

Serious Steak Tacos

*You can barbecue the meat or use up barbecued leftovers.
A real taco needs tons of hot sauce, so pick your favorite and use
enough to make yourself cry... tears of joy, of course. And you'll
never buy a taco at a drive-thru window again.*

Ingredients

1 pound steak

Salt and freshly
ground black pepper

1 teaspoon olive oil

8 taco-sized soft
flour tortillas

8 ounces (1 cup)
shredded Pepper Jack

Hot sauce
(see Hot Sauce List, page 47)

The Steps

1. Season the steak with salt and pepper to taste.

2. Preheat the oven to 450°F.

3. Heat the oil in an ovenproof skillet over medium-high heat.

4. Fry the steak on each side for about 2 minutes. Put the skillet in the oven. Bake for 15 minutes for medium or 20 to 25 minutes for well done (see the box on the opposite page for doneness cues). Remove from the heat and let stand for 3 to 5 minutes to help seal in the juices.

5. Cut the steak into slices and fill the tortillas.

6. Add the cheese and hot sauce to taste.

7. The meat should be warm enough to melt the cheese, but if you like it really melted, stick the tacos on a baking sheet or aluminum foil and bake until the cheese is melted and beginning to bubble, 3 to 4 minutes.

Serves 2

Jerk Chops

These are spicy and delicious. If you can't go to Jamaica, this is the next best thing. Make it Jamaica night and have a Red Stripe beer. You can just as easily grill these, if you're not stuck in an apartment. They are also great with rice.

Ingredients

2 scallions, chopped

2 tablespoons olive oil

5 garlic cloves, chopped

Juice of ½ medium-sized lemon or lime

2 teaspoons honey

1 teaspoon ground allspice

1 teaspoon dried thyme

Salt and freshly ground black pepper

¼ teaspoon ground nutmeg

2 jalapeños, chopped (or 1 habanero for more heat)

1 tablespoon hot sauce
(use the hottest and spiciest you have; see Hot Sauce List on page 47 for options)

4 pork chops (bone-in or bone-out, about 1 inch thick)

The Steps

1. Mix together the scallions, oil, garlic, lemon juice, honey, allspice, thyme, salt and pepper to taste, nutmeg, jalapeños, and hot sauce in a large bowl.

2. Place the pork chops in the bowl and coat well with the sauce. Cover and let the chops marinate in the fridge for a couple of hours.

3. Preheat the oven to 400°F. Get out a medium-sized baking dish and set it aside.

4. Transfer chops from marinade to a large skillet. Reserve marinade. Cook porkchops over high heat for 1 to 2 minutes on each side. (This will brown the chops almost like you actually grilled them.)

5. Place the pork chops in the baking dish with the reserved sauce and bake for 20 minutes, or until the meat is white in the center. Remove from the heat.

6. Let the chops rest for at least 5 minutes to absorb all the juices before serving.

Serves 4

Foil-Wrapped Chicken

This is a great way to have a very tender piece of chicken. Dark meat works better, but you can also use white. The darker the meat, the sweeter the juice. You can skewer the chicken cubes and grill them instead of baking, if desired.

Ingredients

¼ cup low-sodium soy sauce

Juice of 1 medium-sized lemon (about 3 tablespoons)

2 tablespoons Asian hot sauce (Sriracha works best)

Salt and freshly ground black pepper

3 boneless and skinless chicken thighs or breasts (about 2 pounds), cut into 10 cubes

10 squares of aluminum foil, 5" by 5"

The Steps

1. Mix the soy sauce, lemon juice, hot sauce, and salt and pepper to taste in a medium-sized, airtight bowl.

2. Place the chicken cubes in the bowl, cover, and marinate in the fridge for at least 30 minutes. The longer you marinate, the better; overnight works well.

3. Preheat the oven to 450°F.

4. Put one piece of marinated chicken in each foil square and fold to make a triangle. Make sure to seal the sides together so the liquid can't leak out. Discard any excess marinade.

5. Place the foil-wrapped chicken on a baking sheet or dish. Bake for 20 minutes, until the chicken is white in the center. Remove from the oven and let rest for 2 minutes to seal in the juices. Unwrap and eat.

Serves 2

The Essential Hot Sauce List

Hot sauce has quickly replaced most of the other condiments in my kitchen. Why settle for ketchup when you can eat something that might make you cry?

Arizona Gunslinger Smokin' Hot

Atomic Wing Sauce

Blair's Original Death Sauce

Busha Brown's Pukka Hot Pepper Sauce

Cholula Hot Sauce

Frank's Original Red Hot

El Yucateco Green Habenaro Sauce

Hoy Fong Sriracha Garlic Hot Sauce

Iguana Gold Island Pepper Sauce

Jim Beam Hot Sauce

Louisiana Hot Sauce

Marie Sharp's Habanero Pepper and
    Hot Green Habanero sauces

Mild to Wild Smokin'
    Chipotle Sauce

Tabasco

Tapatio

Whoop Ass Hot Sauce

Hawaiian Chicken

While kicking back in Maui, I saw a group of crazy chickens running around a pineapple field. This recipe popped into my head. You can use any part of the chicken — just realize you have to cut it up into bite-sized pieces. Or buy prepackaged pieces of breast meat; it's a lot easier.

Ingredients

2 tablespoons
vegetable oil

1 teaspoon paprika

1 cup flour

2 pounds fryer
chicken, cut into
bite-sized chunks

1 cup pineapple juice

2 tablespoons brown
sugar

1 tablespoon
white wine vinegar

4 fresh basil leaves,
chopped, or
1 teaspoon dried

1 teaspoon
ground nutmeg

1 cup pineapple
chunks

2 cups cooked
white rice

The Steps

1. Heat the oil over medium heat in a large skillet.

2. Combine the paprika and flour in a medium-sized bowl.

3. Lightly coat the chicken in the flour mixture.

4. Sauté the floured chicken, stirring and turning occasionally, until golden brown on all sides, about 10 minutes.

5. Mix the pineapple juice, brown sugar, vinegar, basil, and nutmeg in a separate bowl.

6. Add the juice mixture to the chicken in the skillet and stir.

7. Cover and reduce the heat to low; simmer for 20 to 30 minutes, or until the chicken is white in the center.

8. Add the pineapple chunks and continue to simmer for another 5 minutes. Serve Hawaiian Chicken over rice with all the skillet juices.

Serves 2

Munchie Tip

You can buy pineapple in a can and use both the chunks and the juice. A 16-ounce can will give you enough juice and more than enough fruit. If you are using a fresh pineapple, the chunks of fruit will taste better but you will need to buy extra juice in a can or jar.

Baked Bird with Goldfish Crust

I created this recipe while aimlessly walking down the aisles of the supermarket one late, lonely night.

Ingredients

1 tablespoon
olive oil

1 large egg, beaten

1 bag (6 ounces)
Goldfish crackers,
crushed into
crumbs

2 boneless and
skinless chicken
or turkey breasts

The Steps

1. Preheat the oven to 450°F. Lightly grease a baking dish with the oil so the chicken won't stick.

2. Beat the egg in a bowl.

3. Put the Goldfish crumbs in another bowl.

4. Drench the chicken in the egg, then coat well with the Goldfish crumbs.

5. Bake for 35 to 45 minutes, or until the chicken is white in the center and crispy on the outside.

Serves 2

Easy Crumbs

It's easy to make bread crumbs out of almost any type of cracker, toast, or even pretzels. I spread out the Goldfish (or other crunchy morsel) on a cutting board and use the heels of my hands to crush them. You can also spread them out and cover with a clean dish towel and **hit them all over** with a rolling pin or hammer. Don't get too excited — you just want to break them up, **not turn them into sawdust**. If you are using toast — use stale bread and make sure it is very toasted, dark brown. Try using the thick teeth on a grater or dump it in the blender and pulse it until you have crumbs. Another option is to dump the crackers into a paper or plastic bag and slam the bag against the counter until you have crumbs. These are all good stress relievers.

Beef & Mac Delight

Here's an authentic twist on traditional mac & cheese. The good stuff is so easy to make that I'll bet you never bother with instant again. Even the cheese sauce is easy once you get the hang of it. Besides, powdered cheese sucks! And you don't have to bake this recipe — just mix together and devour.

Ingredients

12 ounces small elbow macaroni, cooked and drained

3 tablespoons butter

1 small onion, chopped

1–5 garlic cloves, minced

1 pound ground beef or ground turkey

1 tablespoon flour

¾ cup milk

1 cup shredded cheese (white Cheddar is best)

3 plum tomatoes, chopped

¼ cup grated Parmesan cheese

Salt and freshly ground black pepper

The Steps

1. Pour the cooked macaroni into a large bowl.

2. Heat 1 tablespoon of the butter in a large saucepan and sauté the onions and garlic over medium heat for 1 minute, stirring often.

3. Add the ground beef and cook, stirring occasionally, for about 15 minutes, until meat is brown and completely cooked. Remove from the saucepan and set aside.

4. Melt the remaining butter in the same saucepan over medium-low heat. Sprinkle the flour into the saucepan and, stirring constantly, dissolve the flour into the butter until you have a thick paste.

5. Slowly add the milk and increase the heat to medium, stirring continuously. The sauce will start to thicken. Add the shredded cheese and stir until it is melted and fully incorporated into the sauce.

6. Remove the cheese sauce from the heat and stir it into the macaroni.

7. Add the beef and mix well.

8. Add the tomatoes, Parmesan, and salt and pepper to taste. Mix everything together.

Serves 2

Mac & Cheese Options

✳ **Cheese:** Use sharp Cheddar, Pepper Jack, Gruyère, or colby, or buy a bag with a combo of shredded cheeses.

✳ **Macaroni:** If you like bigger macaroni, go with that.

✳ **Baking:** For a truly fantastic mac & cheese experience I recommend baking it for 10 minutes in the oven. Just preheat the oven to 450°F and go through all of the steps at left. Save a little of the Parmesan instead of mixing it in. Once you have everything combined, empty it all into a greased baking dish and sprinkle the remaining cheese on top. Stick it in the oven or under the broiler until the top is bubbling and crispy, then serve. You can also reserve the tomato and put that on top instead of mixing it in. If you decide to bake it, make sure to boil the macaroni al dente, which means slightly undercooked. You don't want it to be too soggy.

Chili con Bucky

The chiles are the key to this recipe. When you are at the store, pick five chile peppers different in flavor and heat. They don't all have to burn off your tongue to be flavorful.

Ingredients

3 teaspoons olive oil

1 large onion, chopped

1 green pepper, chopped

5 garlic cloves, chopped

5 assorted chiles, seeded and chopped

1 pound ground turkey

1 pound top sirloin steak, cut into 1-inch cubes

5 Roma tomatoes, chopped

2 cans (16 ounces each) kidney beans, drained

1 can (16 ounces) black beans, drained

1 can (15 ounces) tomato sauce

1 can (6 ounces) tomato paste

6 ounces water

Seasonings of your choice
(see Chili Seasonings on opposite page)

1 small zucchini, chopped

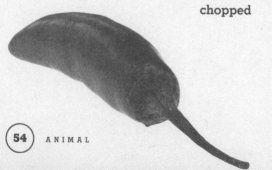

The Steps

1. Heat the oil in a large, heavy-bottomed pot over medium-high heat.

2. Sauté the onions, peppers, garlic, and chiles for about 5 minutes, until the onion is soft and beginning to brown.

3. Add the turkey and steak. Stir and cook for another 5 minutes. You want everything nice and browned.

4. Add the tomatoes, tomato sauce, tomato paste, black beans, and kidney beans. Mix well.

5. Pour 6 ounces of water into the pot. Add the seasonings and cook over medium-high heat, stirring often, for 5 minutes.

6. Once the chili has reached a steady boil, reduce the heat to low. Simmer, covered or uncovered, for 1 hour, stirring every 15 minutes or so. Add zucchini after 30 minutes of cooking. You want to get the chili to a chunky consistency. The liquid will reduce faster if the chili is cooked uncovered, so your cooking time may decrease or you may need to add a little extra water toward the end.

Serves 6

Chili Seasonings

There are so many flavors that make chili great. Everyone seems to have a **favorite secret ingredient.** Once you start cooking chili, you are sure to have an opinion.

Start with about 2 teaspoons of the seasonings you choose and adjust accordingly: chili powder, ground cumin, dried oregano, bay leaf, salt, pepper, hot sauce, garlic powder, cayenne pepper, cinnamon.

Other flavorings are sugar, brown sugar, molasses, and beer. Crumbled smoked bacon or ham adds flavor, whether it is mixed in or sprinkled on top.

Topping Options

* Grated cheese
* Sour cream
* Diced red onion or scallions
* Chopped sweet peppers
* Crumbled crackers or tortilla chips
* Extra jalapeños and hot peppers

Chile Peppers

The hottest parts of a hot pepper are the white membrane and the seeds found inside it. An easy way to cook with hot peppers and control the heat is to remove and discard all the insides and seeds. Or try a hot sauce that uses a specific chile; hot sauce often has ingredients like sugar, vinegar, vegetables, and fruit that cut the heat. Most chile peppers are available fresh, dried, powdered, pickled, and in different condiments — see what you like. Here are a few peppers worth experimenting with.

* **Pickled jalapeños in a can**
* **Fresh red or green jalapeños** — jalapeños are the classic hot pepper. They're great fresh, pickled, or canned, and I use them all.
* **Fresh serrano chilies** — use fresh in salsas or purchase pickled. Use in place of jalapeños for more heat.
* **Chipotle** — basically this just means a smoked pepper, usually jalapeño. Use instead of fresh peppers for a different taste. If you use a hot sauce made with chipotle, you'll find the same smoky flavor.
* **Ancho** — refers to the dried poblano pepper. It's pretty mild and can be canned or powdered.
* **Habanero** — this means hot! Orange and red habaneros are grown in the United States and you might find them in your grocery store. Scotch bonnets are also habaneros.
* **Yellow chile** — use fresh in salsa or with fish.
* **Yellow and red Holland pepper** — another good pepper to use fresh or in salsa.
* **Hot cherry peppers**
* **Red or green Thai chilies**

Chapter 4

Salads

Salads are easy Munchies for those really hot days when the last thing you want to do is turn on anything except the air conditioner. The place I live in has a little wall unit in the far corner that doesn't cool down anything. Even while I sit with ice-packs strapped to my body, scared to go anywhere near the stove, I manage to create these refreshing salads. Salad is also a sophisticated accompaniment to any meal — translation, women eat salad constantly — so keep these in mind when you get to my date recipes.

Spinach Salad with Bacon

*I use Bob's Big Boy Blue Cheese salad dressing with this recipe;
use your favorite. You'll want a creamy, chunky dressing
that gives a nice contrast to the crunchy bacon.*

····· **The Steps**

1. Fry the bacon in a large skillet until crispy, about 10 minutes. Remove from the fat and drain on paper towels. When cool, chop or crumble it.

Ingredients ·······

10 strips bacon

1 bundle spinach (about 1 pound), washed well and coarsely chopped

½ cup blue cheese dressing

2. Mix the bacon, spinach, and dressing in a bowl. Toss and serve.

Serves 1 as a main dish or 2 as a side dish

Egg, Asparagus, Avocado & Tomato Salad

Asparagus gives this salad some crunchy texture while the avocado and egg smooth it out. The tomato is for color as well as taste. Combining the four is a great way to have a lot of contrast in one dish. The Parmesan cheese gives it a nice salty bite.

Ingredients

5 asparagus spears, tough ends trimmed, cut into 3-inch pieces

1 large tomato, diced

1 avocado, peeled, pitted, and cut into chunks

¼ cup grated Parmesan cheese

2 large hard-cooked eggs, sliced or chopped

⅓ cup ranch dressing

Salt and freshly ground black pepper

The Steps

1. Steam the asparagus in ½ inch of water until tender, about 5 minutes. Remove from the water and put in the fridge until chilled.

2. Mix the steamed asparagus, tomato, and avocado in a medium-sized salad bowl.

3. Add the Parmesan, dressing, and salt and pepper to taste. Toss well.

4. Arrange the egg slices on top. Alternatively, you can mix the egg right in with the dressing — this really only works if you've chopped the egg, though.

Serves 1 as a main dish or 2 as a side dish

Warm Asparagus Salad

You can use thick or thin asparagus — the thinner the spear, the younger and tastier it is and the less steaming it needs.

Ingredients

1 pound asparagus spears, tough ends trimmed

2 cups (2 handfuls) mixed greens

1 yellow pepper, chopped

1 avocado, peeled, pitted, and chopped

½ cup creamy Caesar dressing

2 tablespoons Parmesan (if desired)

The Steps

1. Steam the asparagus in ½ inch of water for 3 to 5 minutes, until tender. Set aside.

2. Mix the greens, pepper, and avocado in a large bowl.

3. Lay the steamed asparagus on top of the salad.

4. Sprinkle with the dressing and toss gently. Add the 2 tablespoons of Parmesan to boost the flavor, if you desire.

Serves 2

Dirty Potato Salad

This is the perfect salad when it's hot and you're relaxing. It's dirty because you leave the skins on the potatoes for more flavor and texture. You still have to scrub them, so technically the salad doesn't actually have dirt in it, which is a good thing.

Ingredients

3 pounds Yukon gold potatoes

3 tablespoons white wine vinegar

5 hard-cooked eggs, sliced in half and yolks and whites separated

1 cup mayonnaise

1 small onion, chopped

2 tablespoons yellow mustard

3–5 dill pickles, chopped

2 celery stalks, chopped thin

The Steps

1. Scrub the potatoes but leave the skins on; cut them in half and put them in a large pot with water to cover. Bring to a boil and reduce heat slightly. Cook in gently boiling water, 12 to 15 minutes, or until tender. They should be cooked but not falling apart.

2. Drain; immediately toss with the vinegar in a large bowl.

3. Mash the egg yolks in a separate bowl (save the whites!). Stir in the mayonnaise, onion and mustard.

4. Chop the egg whites and carefully toss with the pickles and celery in a third bowl.

5. Add the egg-celery mixture to the large bowl of potatoes and mix. Gently stir in the yolk mixture, making sure to coat all the potatoes. If the salad is too dry, add a little extra mayonnaise and vinegar.

6. Serve immediately or refrigerate.

About 3½ pounds of salad

Summer Pasta Salad

It's a billion degrees out and you want something light and refreshing. This salad is ideal for a summer barbecue or cookout or just lounging on the couch 2 feet from the air conditioner.

Ingredients

2 cans (6 ounces each) tuna or chicken, drained and chopped

1 green pepper, finely chopped

1 small onion, finely chopped

1 can (12 ounces) black olives, sliced

¾ cup Italian dressing

1 tablespoon mixed Italian herbs

Salt and freshly ground pepper

1 pound pasta cooked, drained, and cooled

(fusili, rotini or fresh tortellini works best)

The Steps

1. Mix the tuna, green pepper, onion, and black olives in a large salad bowl.

2. Add the dressing, mixed herbs, and salt and pepper to taste. Mix well and add the pasta. Toss, cover, and refrigerate for at least 30 minutes before serving.

About 1½ pounds salad; serves 4 as a side dish

ROSEMARY

PARSLEY

THYME

BASIL

OREGANO

Tomato & Cucumber Salad

Nothing could be simpler than this invigorating salad.
Look for small cucumbers — they have fewer seeds.

The Steps

1. Toss the tomatoes, cucumbers, balsamic vinegar, salt, and pepper to taste in a bowl.

2. Serve immediately or refrigerate.

Serves 2

Ingredients

4 Roma tomatoes, chopped into 1-inch pieces

1–2 small cucumbers, chopped into 1-inch pieces, peeled or unpeeled

2 tablespoons balsamic vinegar or Simple Vinaigrette*

1 teaspoon salt

Freshly ground black pepper

Simple Vinaigrette*

½ cup olive oil
2½ tablespoons champagne or red wine vinegar
Salt and freshly ground black pepper, to taste
1½ teaspoons Dijon mustard

Place all the ingredients in a small jar with a tightly fitting lid. Now shake it really hard, but don't go wild unless you are sure the jar is leak-proof. This should incorporate the vinegar and oil and the whole dressing will be thick and nicely blended. Get used to doing this and you can try adding different stuff — dried or fresh herbs and different vinegars like balsamic — or add a pinch of sugar or some minced garlic. The real trick is to use olive oil and shake well.

Toasting Nuts and Seeds

You can use the toaster oven (see my tip in Date Recipes, page 125) or you can do it in a conventional oven or on the stovetop. Some of the best seeds to toast are all those pumpkin seeds after you carve your jack-o'-lantern on Halloween. Most nuts are delicious roasted.

Oven: Preheat to 450°F. Spread out the nuts or seeds in a single layer on a baking sheet. Place the sheet on the highest rack. The cooking time will vary depending on the nuts or seeds you use and their size. Keep checking them and shaking the pan so the nuts roll around and toast on every side. The best way to tell they are done is with your nose. There should be a distinct aroma of roasted nuts. Get them out of the oven and off the pan quickly so they don't burn.

Stovetop: Get a heavy iron skillet nice and hot over a high heat and put the nuts in it. Shake it continually so the nuts roll around and don't burn.

Both of these methods are good for doing lots of nuts; the toaster oven is perfect for smaller jobs.

Mediterranean Salad

Pretend you're in the south of France. This salad beats an international flight with a screaming baby on board any day.

Ingredients

1 can (14 ounces)
artichoke hearts,
in water

1 can (14 ounces)
hearts of palm,
cut into ¼-inch slices

1 can (6 ounces)
crabmeat

2 tablespoons
Dijon mustard

1 tablespoon
balsamic vinegar

3 tablespoons
olive oil

Salt and freshly
ground black
pepper

Bed of lettuce
(if desired)

The Steps

1. To make the salad, gently mix the artichoke hearts, hearts of palm, and crabmeat in a large bowl.

2. To make a mustard balsamic vinaigrette, mix the mustard and balsamic vinegar in a small bowl.

3. Slowly pour the olive oil into the mustard mixture, stirring. This will allow the olive oil to blend with the other ingredients so the dressing becomes nice and creamy.

4. Pour the vinaigrette over the salad, season with the salt and pepper to taste, and mix well.

5. Let the salad meld its flavors for 10 to 30 minutes in the fridge. Serve on a bed of lettuce, if desired, or all by itself.

Serves 1 as a main dish or 2 as a side dish

The Best Taco Salad Ever

It truly is. The flavors are blended so perfectly that I actually eat it every weekend during football season. When my friend Jason Chauncey makes it, no one can get enough.

Ingredients

2 pounds lean
ground beef
(7% fat or less)

2 packets Lawry's
Taco Seasoning

1 head iceberg
lettuce, coarsely
chopped

1 bunch scallions,
thinly sliced

8 ounces (about 1 cup)
shredded Cheddar or
Mexican Blend

1 bottle (16 ounces)
Thousand Island
dressing

(Bob's Big Boy makes
a really good Thousand
Island dressing; it's what
I use but it's available only
on the West Coast)

Toppings (for garnish;
see Options box)

1 large bag
tortilla chips

The Steps

1. Cook the beef in a large skillet over medium to high heat until browned and hot throughout, about 15 minutes. While the beef is still cooking, mix in the taco seasoning and follow the directions on the back of the packet.

2. Set aside the seasoned beef in a bowl to cool, so it won't wilt the lettuce.

3. Toss the cooled beef, lettuce, scallions, cheese, and dressing in a large mixing bowl.

4. Garnish with the toppings of your choice (see Topping Options, below) or serve an assortment on the side.

5. Eat it like a dip with the tortilla chips.

Serves 5

Topping Options

* Sour cream

* Hot sauce (see Hot Sauce List, page 47)

* Salsa

* Diced jalapeños or other hot peppers

* Guacamole

* Canned sweet corn

Asian Cucumber Salad

This recipe is called Sunomono in Japanese. You should use hothouse cucumbers, but regular cucumbers work too and are a lot cheaper. This recipe lasts for days as long as it's covered and refrigerated, so make as much as you want.

Ingredients

2 cucumbers, peeled and sliced thin

½ cup rice vinegar

1 teaspoon sesame oil

Salt and freshly ground black pepper

1 tablespoon toasted sesame seeds
(see Toasting Nuts and Seeds, page 64 or purchase toasted in the spice section of your supermarket)

The Steps

1. Toss the cucumber, rice vinegar, sesame oil, and salt and pepper to taste in a resealable airtight container.

2. Cover and refrigerate. When the salad is chilled and the vinegar has really seeped in, 1 to 2 hours, sprinkle with the toasted sesame seeds.

Serves 1 or 2

Vegetable peeler. This tool is essential. I use it all the time, and I'm always coming up with new things that I can do with it in the kitchen. Get a good one that stays pretty sharp and you won't regret it.

Grater. Ditto. You might think you don't need a little gadget like this when you have a great big knife to do all the work, but it comes in handy for all sorts of things, from shredding cheese to grating spices and chiles. Get one with a slicer so you can make wafer-thin slices of veggies, cheese, or pepperoni whenever you need to.

Both of these tools have the advantage of being easy to use and difficult to do much damage with.

German Potato Salad

German Potato Salad is best served warm or at room temperature.
I live near a German deli, Atlas Sausage in North Hollywood,
where I get this scrumptious salad. I actually begged the owner
to give me the recipe for my book. If you aren't lucky enough to
have a German deli near you, this is a must.

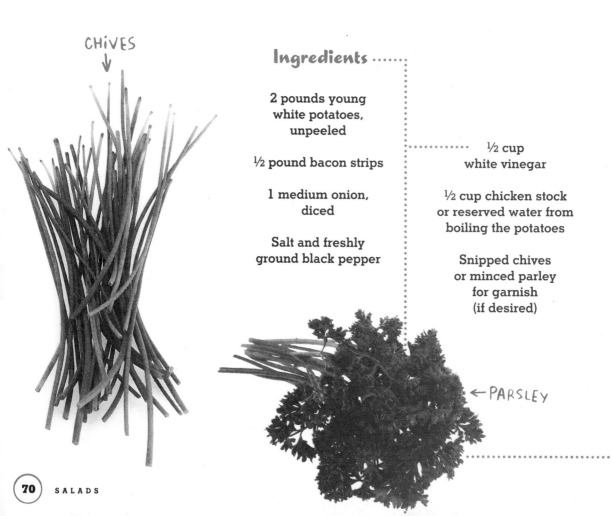

CHIVES

Ingredients

2 pounds young
white potatoes,
unpeeled

½ pound bacon strips

1 medium onion,
diced

Salt and freshly
ground black pepper

½ cup
white vinegar

½ cup chicken stock
or reserved water from
boiling the potatoes

Snipped chives
or minced parley
for garnish
(if desired)

← PARSLEY

The Steps

1. Scrub the potatoes, place in salted water to cover, bring to a boil, and cook in softly boiling water for about 15 minutes, or until tender. Drain.

2. While the potatoes are still hot, skin them and cut them into ¼-inch slices. Set aside in a large salad bowl.

3. Cook the bacon and onion in a large skillet until the bacon is almost crisp and the onion is transparent, 7 or 8 minutes. Remove from the skillet, set aside, and pat bacon dry with paper towels.

4. Drain all but 1 tablespoon of the bacon fat from the skillet.

5. Return the skillet to the burner and add the vinegar and stock. Cook, over medium-low heat, until the mixture is slightly thickened, 8 to 12 minutes.

6. Return the bacon and onion to the skillet and cook for another 2 to 3 minutes, until all ingredients are well combined and hot.

7. Pour this hot dressing over the cooked potatoes, stirring gently to blend.

8. Sprinkle with the chives or parsley (if desired). Serve warm.

About 2 pounds; serves 4

POTATOES →

Must-Have Mustard

All potato salads are great with sausages and spicy mustard; in fact, mustard is good on almost anything. Here are some top picks of one of my favorite condiments:

✻ Ballpark yellow mustard — best for burgers and hotdogs

✻ Classic Dijon — for those upgraded burgers, sausages, and salad dressings

✻ Hot and spicy mustards like Colman's English Mustard, Bone Suckin' Mustard, and Beaver Jalapeño Mustard

✻ German mustards such as Plochman's Hearty Bavarian, Spicy Honey, and Stone Ground

✻ Whole-grain mustards such as Grey Poupon Spicy Brown Mustard and Country Dijon

✻ Horseradish mustards

✻ Maple or honey mustard — fantastic with ham

Chapter 5

Vegetate

I know, I know, everyone hates to eat his veggies. From the littlest kid to the president of the United States. For some reason the "dull weed" is disliked and hardly ever eaten. Wait, hold up! Before you give up entirely, you have to sample some of the recipes I've created. I guarantee these simple dishes will bring life back into your boring veggieless existence. So try some of these delectable vegetable munchies and don't chill out, *veg out.*

Mom's No-Pasta Chunky Minestrone Soup

Soup is great on a rainy day when you're sick and your body is screaming for something healthy. Adding a jalapeño or two spices up this soup nicely. This recipe makes enough to serve four so if it is just you eating, freeze the leftovers or enjoy soup all week.

Ingredients

3 cloves garlic, coarsely chopped

1 large onion, coarsely chopped

3 tablespoons olive oil

2 carrots, coarsely chopped

1 yellow or green pepper, coarsely chopped

½ pound broccoli crowns, coarsely chopped (about 1 cup)

2 celery stalks, coarsely chopped

1 teaspoon dried oregano

1 can (10 ounces) tomato paste

4 cups water or canned broth

1 can (16 ounces) kidney beans, drained and rinsed

Salt and freshly ground black pepper

1 small green zucchini, coarsely chopped

1 small yellow squash, coarsely chopped

The Steps

1. Sauté the garlic and onion in olive oil in your largest pot over medium heat until the onion starts to become transparent, about 5 minutes.

2. Add the carrots, pepper, broccoli, celery, and oregano and sauté for another 5 minutes.

3. Add the tomato paste and water; bring to a boil.

4. Add the kidney beans, stir, and return to a boil. If the soup looks too thick, you may need to add a little more water. Season with salt and pepper.

5. Turn the heat to low, cover, and simmer, stirring occasionally, for 45 minutes to 1 hour. Add the zucchini and yellow squash for the final 30 minutes of cooking. The soup should look nice and chunky and the vegetables tender but not pale and falling apart. Taste and adjust seasoning.

Serves 4

Soup Topping Options

❋ Sprinkle with chopped onion, parsley, or fresh herbs.

❋ Grate some Parmesan or Gruyère cheese on top. Squeeze a little lemon over each bowl — this is really good if you are sick.

❋ Croutons or diced tomatoes will add crunch and flavor, as will some crumbled bacon.

❋ Sprinkle with hot pepper flakes or your favorite hot sauce.

Soup Tips

When you make soup, try to use vegetable, beef, or chicken broth instead of water. You can purchase it in cans in the supermarket, usually right next to the soup. It is worth using the low-sodium variety and adding more salt if needed.

Another option that will make your soup more flavorful is to add a bouillon cube if you are using water. These are little cubes of concentrated beef, chicken, or vegetable flavoring — add as many as you need according to the amount of water you are using.

Here's another flavor booster: Sauté some chopped bacon with the vegetables.

Adding sage, 1 teaspoon dried or a few chopped fresh leaves, will give your soup a robust, smoky flavor. You'll feel like you're out on the range in front of a campfire instead of at home sick.

Roasted Asparagus

Roasting vegetables is very Euro. You can use thin or thick asparagus spears. The cooking time will vary: The thicker the spear, the more cooking it will need.

Ingredients

1 rubber-band bundle asparagus (1 pound, 16 to 20 spears), bottoms trimmed

1 teaspoon olive oil

½ teaspoon salt

½ teaspoon dried thyme

The Steps

1. Preheat oven to 450°F. Line a baking sheet with foil.

2. Wash the asparagus and arrange in a single layer on the baking sheet.

3. Drizzle the oil over the asparagus.

4. Sprinkle with the salt and thyme. Roll the spears around to make sure they are coated.

5. Roast in the oven for 20 to 25 minutes, or until tender.

Serves 1 as a main dish or 2 as a side dish

Shanghai Cabbage

Cabbage is the reason that Asians live longer than Americans. Also known as bok choy, this dark leafy green helps keep the cancer away. There are both large heads of bok choy and baby heads.

Ingredients

1 tablespoon butter

1 head bok choy (or 2 baby heads), rinsed well

Juice of half a lemon (about 1½ tablespoons)

½ teaspoon salt

The Steps

1. Melt the butter in a large skillet over medium-high heat.

2. Cut the bok choy leaves crosswise in thirds and place in the skillet.

3. Sprinkle with the lemon juice and salt.

4. Sauté, stirring frequently, 5 to 7 minutes, until slightly brown and wilted.

5. Eat and kick some cancer butt!

Serves 1 as a main dish or 2 as a side dish

Potato Pancakes

These pancakes are great in the morning, afternoon, or evening.

Ingredients

2 large russet potatoes, scrubbed, and peeled

Juice of ⅓ medium-sized lemon (about 1 tablespoon)

1 small onion, shredded

2 large eggs

1½ tablespoons flour

Salt and freshly ground black pepper

2 tablespoons olive oil

The Steps

1. Using the large holes on your grater, thickly shred the potatoes and onion.

2. Cover the potatoes with water, add the lemon juice, and soak them for a few minutes. (This will eliminate some of the starch and keep them from turning brown.) Drain and pat dry.

3. Mix the potatoes, onion, eggs, flour, and salt and pepper to taste in a bowl. Form patties with your hands; you should get four palm-sized patties.

4. Heat the oil in a large skillet. Fry the potato patties until golden brown, about 8 minutes on each side.

5. Pat the pancakes with paper towels to remove excess oil, then keep them warm in the oven or toaster oven.

Serves 2

Serve It Up

* Sour cream

* Nanny's Homemade Applesauce (page 142)

Zucchini Boats

Growing up, we had a small garden, and the only thing Mom was able to grow was zucchini. Just my luck. It's every kid's nightmare to have to eat as much zucchini as I did, and to eat it prepared in every way imaginable. If you have grown to like zucchini, however, you'll love this recipe.

Ingredients

2 teaspoons butter

4 cloves garlic, minced

4 zucchini, halved lengthwise

½ cup shredded Cheddar or Monterey Jack

The Steps

1. Preheat the oven to 400°F.

2. Melt the butter in an ovenproof skillet over medium-high heat. Sauté the garlic for 1 to 2 minutes, until it smells great but is not yet browning.

3. Add the zucchini halves and sauté for another 2 minutes. Make sure both sides of the zucchini are well sautéed and slightly brown.

4. Remove the skillet from the heat. Set the zucchini skin-side down and spread the cheese evenly on all eight halves.

5. Put the skillet in the oven and bake for 6 to 8 minutes, or until the zucchini halves are tender and the cheese is melted.

6. Turn the oven to broil and cook for another minute, or until the cheese topping is bubbling and crispy.

Serves 2 as a main dish or 4 as a side dish

50/50 Artichokes

If you don't own a vegetable steamer, here's a great way to cook artichokes: half boiling and half steaming — 50/50. Artichokes and mayo are perfect together. Another option is melted butter.

Ingredients

4 artichokes of any size

Dipping Options

✳ ¼ cup mayonnaise

✳ ½ teaspoon chili powder or paprika mixed in mayonnaise

✳ 1 clove minced garlic mixed in mayonnaise

✳ 2 tablespoons melted butter

✳ Freshly squeezed lemon juice, on its own or added to the butter

✳ Ranch or Caesar dressing

The Steps

1. Wash and trim the stem ends of the artichokes so they have a flat base and stand on their own. You can also trim the very tops with scissors and pull off the toughest bottom leaves.

2. Select a pot that comfortably fits all four artichokes. Fill it with just enough water to cover the artichokes halfway (50 percent); bring to a boil.

3. Cover and cook at a low boil for 30 minutes, turning over the artichokes with tongs after 15 minutes. (This allows the artichokes to be boiled and steamed.) To tell when they're done, pull off one of the leaves — it should come off with no problem and be very tender. If they need more than 30 minutes, have no fear, I've never overcooked an artichoke in my life.

Serves 2 as a main dish or 4 as a side dish

How to Eat It

You can eat all of the leaves of an artichoke. Just keep pulling them off; dip in the butter, mayo, or dressing of your choice; and scrape leaf against your teeth. You can't actually chew and swallow a whole leaf, so don't try. When you get down to the heart, the leaves will be incredibly tender and you can eat these whole. DON'T try to eat the prickly stuff around the heart; cut it away and eat just the tender heart — it is usually a strange grayish green color. It's delicious dipped in lemony butter or garlicky mayo. If you have an iron will, save the hearts and refrigerate them. Chopped, they are great in salads or on pizza.

EAt
THiS
END

Baked Veggies

Use your favorite vegetables or what is in season for this easy comfort dish. Baked veggies are the perfect side dish with all meats and most fish and are delicious on their own.

The Steps

1. Preheat the oven to 375°F. Line a large baking sheet, or roasting pan if you have one, with aluminum foil.

2. Place the veggies on the baking sheet.

3. Dot the veggies with the butter and sprinkle with the lemon juice, salt, and the pepper to taste.

4. Wrap the veggies in the foil and bake on the sheet — this is in case the juices leak — for 30 to 45 minutes, or until tender. The time will depend on the type of veggies you are cooking.

Serves 1 as a main dish or 2 as a side dish

Ingredients

1 pound assorted vegetables, cut up into roughly the same sizes
(see opposite page)

2 tablespoons butter

Juice of ½ medium-sized lemon (about 1½ tablespoons)

¼ teaspoon salt

Freshly ground black pepper

Eat Your Veggies — the Options

You can bake almost any veggie. The trick is to get a nice variety in terms of color and texture as well as cooking time. Root vegetables like potatoes, yams, sweet potatoes, carrots, squash, beets, and turnips are all great for baking. They'll take a little longer than a softer vegetable like summer squash or bell peppers. Brussels sprouts bake well and taste much better than those boiled ones you get at Thanksgiving. Onions are delicious baked and they add flavor to everything; so does eggplant. **Don't worry if your veggies start to brown** — that happens when the sugars caramelize — the end result will taste great. Most veggies are done when they are tender all the way through. With peppers, the skins will have started to shrivel and wrinkle. Eggplant is cooked when it has collapsed and the skin has become very soft.

If you find a vegetable at the grocery store, in a garden, or in your fridge that you don't know what to do with, **chances are you can bake or roast it with success.** For added flavor, mix in fresh herbs like thyme and rosemary with the veggies or substitute olive oil for the butter.

Cal's Cheesy Cauliflower

In the Midwest they call cheese French dressing. My buddy Cal promises that you won't find this recipe in France.

Ingredients

1 head cauliflower, about 1 pound

1 jar (15 ounces) Cheez Whiz

(or if you are feeling gourmet, about 1½ cups grated Cheddar)

Salt and freshly ground pepper

The Steps

1. Cut the cauliflower into manageable pieces and place in a large pan or pot. Fill with enough water to cover and steam for 20 to 25 minutes, or until tender.

2. Remove from the heat, drain, and place in large bowl.

3. Heat the Cheez Whiz in a saucepan or nuke it according to the package directions.

4. Pour the cheese over the cauliflower, season with salt and pepper, and enjoy.

Serves 2 as a main dish or 4 as a side dish

Fried Mushrooms

Fried mushrooms are a great snack or appetizer. They are also good with a big, greasy, fried breakfast.

Ingredients

1 egg, beaten until smooth

½ cup bread crumbs

1 tablespoon freshly grated Parmesan

Salt and freshly ground black pepper

3 tablespoons vegetable oil

2 cloves garlic, minced

¼ teaspoon dried oregano

12 small mushrooms (white or baby porto-bellos work well)

The Steps

1. Whisk the egg in a bowl.

2. In another bowl, mix the bread crumbs, Parmesan, and salt and pepper to taste.

3. Heat the oil in a large skillet over medium heat.

4. Sauté the garlic and oregano for 2 to 3 minutes, until they produce an aroma but are not yet browning.

5. Coat the mushrooms with the egg, then the bread crumbs. Fry the breaded mushrooms in the skillet for 7 to 10 minutes, turning occasionally. When they're brown and crispy, they're done. If you poke them, they should be tender and release some juice. Drain excess oil on paper towels.

Serves 2

Cleaning Tip
Use a paper towel or napkin to gently brush any dirt from the mushrooms so you don't have to wash with water any longer than necessary. Water is not the mushroom's friend.

Baked Garlic Fries

Get out the Altoids for this one. You can cut the potatoes into wedges or go old school and cut them into ¼-inch strips, just like fast-food fries. You have to cook the potatoes first, so give yourself enough time.

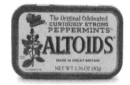

Ingredients

2 large russet potatoes, peeled and cut into wedges or ¼-inch strips

2 tablespoons vegetable oil

½ teaspoon salt, more if you're a salt junkie

1 tablespoon butter

10 cloves garlic, minced

1 tablespoon parsley, fresh or dried (minced if fresh)

3 tablespoons freshly grated Parmesan

The Steps

1. Preheat the oven to 400°F.

2. Combine the potato wedges, oil, and salt in a bowl and mix to coat well.

3. Arrange the potatoes in a single layer on a baking sheet. Bake for 30 to 40 minutes, or until tender. Remove from the oven but leave the oven on!

4. Heat the butter and garlic in a skillet over low heat. Stir until the butter is melted.

5. Add the baked fries to the skillet and stir to coat.

6. Sprinkle the parsley and Parmesan over the coated fries and stir to coat.

7. Turn the oven to broil, put the coated fries back on the baking sheet, and broil until nice and crispy, another 3 to 5 minutes.

Serves 2

What to Dip Your Fries In

❋ Dip in ketchup or hot sauce (see page 47) mixed with 1 table-spoon of cayenne.

❋ Go Belgian and dip fries in mayo. This is much better than it sounds and you can perk up the mayo with different flavors.

❋ Dip in MORE garlic by mixing a chopped garlic clove in ½ cup of mayonnaise.

❋ Sprinkle with 1 tablespoon of freshly squeezed lemon juice (about ⅓ medium-sized lemon) or Worcestershire sauce.

❋ Season with 1 tablespoon of curry powder.

❋ Mix 1 teaspoon of cayenne, paprika, or your favorite hot sauce into ½ cup of mayo and dip.

❋ Top with extra chopped parsley and add a teaspoon or two of balsamic vinegar to ½ cup of mayo to use as a dip.

❋ Sprinkle with malt vinegar and salt in the English style or lime juice and chili powder.

❋ Dip in homemade Thousand Island dressing. To make it, mix equal parts each ketchup, relish, and mayo.

Mushroom & Potato au Gratin

Au gratin means a cooked dish with a melted cheese crust. I wish I could eat everything au gratin. Shallots are just small onions, so don't trip. Try this dish with sour cream.

Ingredients

2 tablespoons olive oil

10 medium-sized mushrooms (about 1½ cups), chopped

5 shallots, chopped

Salt and freshly ground black pepper

5 russet potatoes, cleaned and sliced ¼ inch thick or thinner

16 ounces (about 2 cups) shredded Cheddar

1 bunch scallions (green and white parts), chopped

The Steps

1. Preheat the oven to 425°F. Lightly grease a baking dish.

2. Heat the oil over medium-high heat in a large, heavy-bottomed skillet.

3. Sauté the mushrooms, shallots, and salt and pepper to taste for 3 to 5 minutes, stirring frequently.

4. Arrange half of the potatoes on the bottom of the baking dish. Cover the potatoes with half the mushroom mixture. Cover the mushroom mixture with half of the cheese. Repeat the layering process, ending with cheese on top.

5. Cover with aluminum foil and bake for 30 minutes. Remove the foil and bake an additional 20 minutes. This gets the cheese nice and crispy and browned on top — hence au gratin.

6. Remove from the oven and sprinkle with the scallions.

Serves 2

Chapter 6

The 'Cue

A great opportunity to invite some friends over and impress them with your cooking skills. I say B.Y.O.S. (Bring Your Own Steak), which means you are not stuck shelling out for all the food but you still get to be the gracious host. Most of these recipes are for one steak, so adjust the seasonings or marinades if you are cooking more than that. What's great about barbecuing is that if you accidentally burn something, you can just call it "blackened." That is the hip term for basically burning your food. Except restaurants do it on purpose and charge you for it.

Beer-Soaked Steak

What kind of beer should you use? I use what I'm already drinking. But if you want to get fancy, try Guinness or a bitter beer. Choose your favorite cut of steak.

Ingredients

1 can or bottle (12 ounces) beer

1 pound steak, your favorite cut

1–5 garlic cloves, chopped

2 sprigs rosemary

Salt and freshly ground black pepper

The Steps

1. Pour the beer into a container big enough to hold it and the steak.

2. Prick both sides of the steak with a fork a few times. Marinate it in the beer for at least 30 minutes in the fridge.

3. Remove from the fridge and add the garlic, rosemary, and salt and pepper to taste.

4. Grill until desired doneness.

Serves 1

Searing

Searing is a cooking technique that you can use with all kinds of meat. It browns the meat and helps lock in juices and flavor. It's fun because you do it over a really high heat and it makes lots of cool sizzling noises and smells fantastic. To sear something, heat up a heavy skillet over high heat. Using a large serving fork, stab the piece of meat and place it in the skillet. Let it cook on each side for about 3 minutes, or until it is definitely browned. As each side browns, reposition the meat with your fork until the entire cut is done. At this point your meat is ready for whatever cooking method you are planning to subject it to next. Note that searing is not a substitute for cooking; in many cases the meat is still totally raw and cold inside. The exception to this is when you sear certain types of fish — tuna, for instance — as a way of cooking them.

Grilled Veggies

This simple and healthful recipe goes great with any main dish. You can use any vegetables in season. Slice them and wrap in foil (as the recipe calls for) or chop them and stick them on skewers. If you use skewers, mushrooms and baby eggplant work well.

Ingredients

1 green pepper, sliced into 2- to 3-inch strips

1 yellow pepper, sliced into 2- to 3-inch strips

1 summer squash, sliced into 2- to 3-inch strips

1 zucchini, sliced into 2- to 3-inch strips

1 tablespoon olive oil

3–5 cloves garlic, minced

Salt and freshly ground black pepper

The Steps

1. Mix the peppers, squash, and zucchini in a large bowl.

2. Mix the oil and garlic in a separate, small bowl.

3. Drizzle the oil mixture onto the vegetables. Season with the salt and pepper to taste.

4. Wrap the seasoned veggies in aluminum foil and place directly on the grill.

5. Grill for 20 minutes, or until the veggies are nice and soft.

Serves 2

Drunken Chicken

What's great about this recipe is that it's the chicken that gets intoxicated. The longer you can marinate it in the beer, the more flavor it will absorb. This is a great time to experiment with different types of beers and create different flavors for the chicken. You can use any part of the chicken you like. Stubb's Chicken Marinade goes perfectly with this recipe.

The Steps

1. Pour the beer into a large bowl. Add the chicken, marinade, garlic, rosemary, and salt and pepper to taste. Mix well. Cover and refrigerate for at least an hour.

2. When you're ready, place the chicken on the grill. Turn it so that it browns on each side. Cook until crispy and the outside is slightly blackened and the meat inside white, 8 to 12 minutes per side.

Serves 2-4

Ingredients

1 bottle of light or amber beer

5–8 pieces chicken (about 1½–2 pounds)

½ cup Stubb's Chicken Marinade

5–10 cloves garlic, minced

2–5 sprigs rosemary

Salt and freshly ground black pepper

Honey Cayenne Pepper Steak

The honey and pepper give your meat a sweet and spicy flavor. Use any cut of meat you like.

Ingredients

2 tablespoons honey

2 tablespoons cayenne pepper

1 pound steak, any cut

The Steps

1. Heat the honey and cayenne in a large skillet over low heat, stirring often.

2. Prick both sides of the steak with a fork a few times. This helps the steak absorb the seasoning.

3. When the honey starts to get thin and a little watery, add the steak to the skillet.

4. Increase the heat a little and sear the steak for 3 minutes on each side. Let all the flavors infuse the steak.

5. Transfer the steak from the skillet to the grill and grill for an additional 10 to 12 minutes, or until desired doneness (see box on page 42).

Serves 1

Atomic Wings

My friend Mike Simko and I make these when our group of friends get together for a sports event. He makes the sauce and I sweat over the barbecue, usually missing half the game because our friends always want them crispier.

The Steps

Ingredients

4 pounds chicken wings (or a combo of wings and drumettes)

4 tablespoons (½ stick) butter

½–1 bottle Frank's Red Hot Sauce

Secret Ingredient

To make these babies nuclear, you need to add 3 to 5 droppers of Quaker Steak and Lube Atomic Wing Sauce. It actually comes in an eyedropper and has a release form. Check out Cool Products (page 180) for all the info.

1. Boil the chicken in a large pot of water for 15 to 20 minutes, until the meat is cooked, white and fleshy. Remove from heat and drain.

2. Grill the chicken until crispy, 15 to 25 minutes. The meat will be golden brown with slightly blackened edges.

3. Melt the butter in a large bowl in the microwave. Start with 30 seconds and check every 10 seconds thereafter.

4. Add the Frank's Red Hot to the butter and mix. Squirt the Atomic Wing Sauce into the bowl. Add the wings and mix well.

Serves 4

Other Sauce Options

✳ Stubb's Moppin' Sauce

✳ Tapatio and melted butter

✳ Arizona Gunslinger

✳ Cholulo and melted butter

Killer Shark Tacos

Don't feed these to Steven Spielberg. He is superstitious about eating shark since he filmed Jaws. "If I don't eat them, they won't eat me," he says. Local surfers never eat shark before they grab the stick. For you landlubbers, have no fear, the killer shark is here.

Ingredients

2 tablespoons olive oil

1 pound shark fillets

Salt and freshly ground black pepper

Juice of 1 lemon (about 3 tablespoons)

1 medium-sized head of cabbage, finely chopped

1 can (12 ounces) refried beans

8 taco-sized (corn or flour) soft tortillas

Hot sauce, enough to leave you gasping

(see Hot Sauce List, page 47)

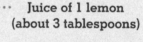

Cooking-the-Shark Steps

1. Rub the olive oil on both sides of the shark fillets.

2. Season with the salt and pepper to taste.

3. Grill the fillets for 5 to 7 minutes on each side, or until crispy and flaky. While grilling, squeeze the lemon over the fillets.

4. Place the fillets on a plate and cut into ½-inch strips.

Final Steps

5. Chop the cabbage and put in a bowl.

6. Pour the beans into a separate microwave-safe bowl and nuke according to the instructions on the can.

7. Heat the tortillas over a burner or in a toaster oven until they are warm but not toasted.

8. Spread the cooked beans on the warm tortillas. Add the sliced fillets, cabbage, and hot sauce to taste. Fold and eat.

Serves 2 (4 each)

Is This Done?

The best way to tell if fish is done (and this applies to meat as well) is its temperature. It should be HOT inside. It should be hot at the thickest part of the cut. Another good way of testing for fish doneness is to see whether it flakes when you cut it. The flesh should easily flake apart and appear opaque and white. If it is still clear or slightly pink, it isn't done. (Okay, salmon will always look pink, but it will be flaky and opaque too.)

Barbecued Ribs

*Here's a perfect recipe to break open that special barbecue sauce.
Use your favorite or the one you've been dying to try.*

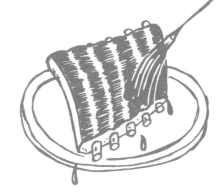

Ingredients

1 slab baby-back
ribs, cut into 2–4
rib pieces each
(about 12–14 ribs
per slab)

1 cup barbecue
sauce

1 jalapeño, minced

1 tablespoon
brown sugar

1 tablespoon
chili powder

½ teaspoon cumin

Juice of ½ medium-
sized lemon (about
1½ tablespoons)

Salt and freshly
ground black
pepper

The Steps

1. Put ribs in a large pot and fill with enough water to cover them. Bring to a boil and reduce heat to simmer. Cook, uncovered, for 30 minutes.

2. Meanwhile, mix the barbecue sauce, jalapeño, brown sugar, chili powder, cumin, lemon juice, and salt and pepper to taste in a medium-sized bowl.

3. Drain the ribs and pat dry.

4. Drench the cooked ribs in the sauce bowl.

5. Grill the ribs for 20 to 30 minutes, until the sauce has formed a nice glaze and the ribs are dark. You can keep brushing on sauce as the ribs grill.

Serves 2

'Cue Tips

If you're stuck with buying one of those little portable barbecues (for lack of space or money), Weber makes a good one. A barbecue of this size will work, but it will take a little longer.

If you just flat out don't have access to a barbecue (which probably means you are a mole and live underground), you can always cook on the stovetop or bake these recipes.

Prep Your 'Cue

You do have to preheat a barbecue. It takes 20 to 30 minutes to prepare charcoal; you want it to look like clumps of white ash before you cook over it. It takes only about 5 minutes to preheat a gas grill turned way up. Keep this in mind when following the recipes in this chapter — be sure to allow yourself enough time.

Essential BBQ Sauces

❄ Bull's-Eye Original BBQ Sauce

❄ Sweet Baby Ray's Barbecue Sauce

❄ Stubb's Original Bar-B-Q Sauce

❄ Southern Comfort Bar-B-Cue Sauce

❄ Lea & Perrins Barbecue Sauce

❄ Kona Coast Bar-B-Cue Sauce

❄ Texas Best "Original Rib Style" Barbecue Sauce

❄ Kraft "Slow Simmered" Original Barbecue Sauce

❄ Grill Mates

❄ Jack Daniels BBQ Sauce

❄ Bone Suckin' Sauce

❄ KC Masterpiece Original Barbecue Sauce

Simple Grilled Salmon

When you get tired of other kinds of meat, salmon is easy to grill. Quick lesson on salmon. It contains omega-3 oils. These are oils that are good for your heart. So it helps prevent heart attacks. Heart attacks are a bad vibe.

Ingredients

1 teaspoon olive oil

1-pound salmon fillet

1 teaspoon Old Bay Seasoning

Salt and freshly ground black pepper

Juice of ½ medium-sized lemon (about 1½ tablespoons)

1 teaspoon butter

The Steps

1. Rub the oil on both sides of the salmon so it won't stick to the grill.

2. Season with the Old Bay and salt and pepper to taste.

3. Grill flesh-side down first, so the last of the grilling happens with the skin on the grill.

4. Grill about 8 minutes on each side, or until fish is pink and flaky.

5. Remove the salmon from the barbecue, drizzle with lemon juice, and rub with the butter.

Serves 1 or 2

Ponzu Chicken

Ponzu sauce now comes in a bottle. It makes life a lot easier. If you can't find it, I've included a recipe (below) that will get you by. You don't need to add salt because the soy sauce is full of it.

Ingredients

½ bottle Ponzu sauce or ½ cup homemade Ponzu Sauce*

1 chile (as hot as you like), sliced thin

1 tablespoon fresh ginger, peeled and minced

1–5 cloves garlic, minced

2 teaspoons sugar

Freshly ground black pepper

Juice of ½ lime (about 1 tablespoon)

4–8 pieces chicken, whatever parts you want or have (about 1½–2 pounds)

The Steps

1. Heat the Ponzu sauce, chile, ginger, garlic, sugar, black pepper to taste, and lime juice in a saucepan over low heat, stirring, until the sugar dissolves, 3 to 4 minutes. Remove from the heat and pour into a large bowl.

2. Add the chicken to the bowl, cover, and marinate for 30 minutes in the fridge.

3. Grill the marinated chicken until crispy and white in the center, about 20 minutes, depending on the size of the chicken pieces.

Serves 2

Ponzu Sauce*

Juice of 2 medium-sized lemons (about 6 tablespoons)
½ cup low-sodium soy sauce
1 teaspoon rice vinegar
Freshly ground black pepper

Mix the ingredients in a small bowl, or shake in a tightly lidded jar, until well blended.

Blackened Pork Chops

Swine is very tasty when done right: crispy on the outside and juicy on the inside.

The Steps

1. Mix the wine, balsamic vinegar, brown sugar, garlic, and salt and pepper to taste in a large bowl.

2. Add the pork chops, cover, and marinate for at least 30 minutes in the fridge.

3. Grill over the highest heat you can without burning the house down, until the pork chops are crispy, blackened, and white in the center, 6 to 8 minutes on each side.

Serves 2

Ingredients

⅓ cup dry red table wine

1 tablespoon balsamic vinegar

½ tablespoon brown sugar

5 cloves garlic, minced

Salt and freshly ground black pepper

2 large pork chops (about ¾ pound each)

Chapter 7

Denizens of the Deep

I know it sounds like a scary ocean movie, but it's just a fancy name for seafood. You can't be scared of cooking fish. It's not hard and takes less time than you think. I'm going to start you off slow. Baby steps. The first recipe in this section is Fish Sticks. If you can make them, you can cook any other fish. It's that simple. You're just substituting a frozen fish stick with a nice fresh piece of fish. Everything else stays pretty much the same. Eat fish — it might be the secret to a long life. I bet you never thought the fountain of youth had anything to do with fish sticks!

The Real Fish Stick

Lots of people will eat fish only in the form of fish sticks. Though this is a fairly limited worldview, I will concede that there is nothing like a nice salty, crispy little stick with tartar sauce! I told you we would start out easy, so get ready to make fish sticks with real fish.

Ingredients

¾ cup finely ground cornmeal plus 2 table-spoons flour (or ¾ cup flour, but cornmeal is crunchier)

1 teaspoon cayenne pepper

4–6 small white fish fillets

½ cup milk or buttermilk

Salt and freshly ground black pepper

3 tablespoons olive oil

Lemon slices and tarter sauce (see opposite page)

The Steps

1. Mix the cornmeal mixture with the cayenne.

2. Pat the fillets dry and dip them in the milk. Season with the salt and pepper to taste.

3. Dredge the fillets in the cornmeal mixture.

4. Heat the oil in a large, heavy-bottomed skillet over medium-high heat.

5. When the skillet is hot but not smoking, add the fillets and fry 3 to 4 minutes on each side, until crispy. Cooking time may vary depending on the size of the fillets, but you'll know they're done when they're hot in the center and flake easily with a fork.

6. Remove from the skillet and drain on paper towels. Eat immediately with lemon and tartar sauce.

Serves 2

Just mix the ingredients together and you're on your way to tartar sauce heaven.

Spicy Herb Tartar Sauce

⅔ cup mayonnaise
1 tablespoon drained capers
1 tablespoon chopped cilantro
1 tablespoon chopped
    jalapeño
1 tablespoon chopped
    fresh parsley
1 tablespoon sweet relish
½ tablespoon freshly
    squeezed lime juice
½ teaspoon Worcestershire
    sauce

Cocktail Sauce

½ cup ketchup
1 tablespoon horseradish
½ tablespoon red wine vinegar
Dash of Tabasco sauce

Basic Tartar Sauce

½ cup mayonnaise
¼ cup sweet relish or
    chopped pickles
1 tablespoon chopped fresh dill
    or 1 teaspoon dried
1 tablespoon Dijon mustard
1 tablespoon freshly squeezed
    lemon juice

Hot Tartar Sauce

⅔ cup mayonnaise
¼ cup chopped sweet pickles
    or relish
1 tablespoon minced hot chiles
    of your choice
2 teaspoons hot sauce
    (see Hot Sauce List, page 47)
1 teaspoon horseradish
1 teaspoon lemon juice

Super Tuna Melt

Here's my twist on the classic. My school lunches sucked too! But my friend Eric Smith lived a block away from the school, so we would sneak away at lunch and make these delicious melts. Occasionally, we would get caught climbing the fence and had to clean windows after school with Lisa Marie Presley, but it was worth it.

Ingredients

2 cans (6 ounces each) tuna, drained

4 tablespoons mayonnaise

2 teaspoons mustard

2 teaspoons Lawry's Pinch of Herbs or other herb blend

4 slices bread of your choice

4 slices cheese of your choice

Salt and freshly ground black pepper

Secret Ingredient

8 sweet pickles, served whole as garnish or chopped and mixed in with the tuna

The Steps

1. Preheat the oven or toaster oven to 350°F.

2. Break up the tuna with a spoon in a small mixing bowl.

3. Stir in the mayonnaise, mustard, and mixed herbs.
Mix thoroughly.

4. Spread the tuna equally on all slices of bread.
Lay the cheese on top of the tuna.

5. Bake on a piece of aluminum foil for 10 minutes,
or until the cheese is melted and the bread is brown.

6. Garnish with the sweet pickles or, if you're desperate,
regular pickles.

Makes 4 open-face sandwiches

Crispy Shrimp Quesadillas

Don't be scared of cooking shrimp — it's like bite-sized chicken with shells and antennae. You can eat these with sour cream, guacamole, salsa, or hot sauce. Or go big like me and use all three. The trick is to get the quesadillas really crispy.

Ingredients

2 tablespoons butter

1 pound medium-sized shrimp, peeled and deveined

1 small onion, thinly sliced

Salt and freshly ground black pepper

5 or 6 large flour tortillas

8 ounces grated Cheddar cheese

The Steps

1. Melt 1 tablespoon of the butter in a large skillet over medium-high heat.

2. Sauté the shrimp, onions, and salt and pepper to taste for 3 to 4 minutes. Flip the shrimp and cook another 3 to 4 minutes, or until they are nice and pink. The onion should be soft. Set on a plate.

3. Keep the skillet on the stovetop. Reduce the heat to medium and melt the remaining butter.

4. Lay a tortilla flat in the skillet. Add some of the cooked shrimp and onion and some of the cheese to half of the tortilla. Cook open for 1 minute, then fold over the tortilla, forming a half-circle.

5. Continue to cook another 3 to 5 minutes, until the tortilla gets golden brown and crispy. Flip and repeat. If you have a large skillet, you can cook two at a time.

Serves 2 or 3

For all you wanna-be expensive plastic surgeons,

deveining shrimp is good practice for removing varicose veins. If you are squeamish about little crustaceans, don't do this at home.

Using a small, sharp knife, slice along the outside curve of the shrimp. You just want to make a slit, not cut the shrimp or your hand in half, so be gentle. Pull out the dark vein and rinse the shrimp with cold water.

You can cook shrimp with the shells on or off and there is no need to remove the little tail before cooking or serving.

When you buy raw shrimp with the shells on, remember that the shells are part of the weight. You will lose about ½ pound from 2 pounds of shrimp once shelled. The best way to plan on how much shrimp to cook is by count rather than weight, unless you buy them already shelled.

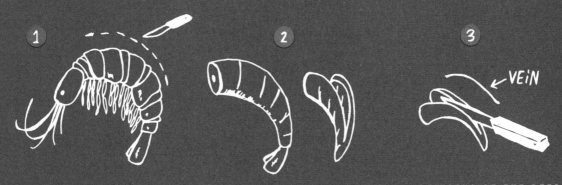

Crab Cakes

No imitations allowed. Be a leader, not a follower. You can serve these with eggs or eat them on their own or in a sandwich. Try mixing cayenne pepper into mayo or ketchup for a spicy dip. Or use one of the tartar sauces on page 105.

Ingredients

1 can (8 ounces) crabmeat

1 large egg, beaten until smooth

½ cup bread crumbs

Salt and freshly ground black pepper

1 tablespoon butter

Sauce Option

1 teaspoon mayonnaise

1 teaspoon ketchup mixed with ¼ teaspoon cayenne pepper

The Steps

1. With your hands, mix the crabmeat, egg, bread crumbs, and salt and pepper to taste in a bowl until well blended.

2. Shape the mixture into two golf balls, then flatten them into 1-inch-thick patties.

3. Melt the butter in a medium-sized skillet over medium-high heat.

4. Fry the patties until golden brown, 3 to 5 minutes on each side.

5. Eat with the sauce option on this page or a tartar sauce of your choice.

Serves 1

Albacore Tataki

Tataki means "lightly cooked" and you use the Almighty Albacore fish, which is the lightest tuna. This is my favorite recipe because it really brings out the flavor of this fish. It's also another great reason to use Ponzu sauce. You must use absolutely fresh fish.

Ingredients

10 garlic cloves, minced

3 scallions, minced

½ cup low-sodium soy sauce

1 tablespoon rice vinegar

Juice of 1 lemon (about 3 tablespoons)

Salt and freshly ground black pepper

1 pound albacore steaks

Steps to Make the Kicked-Up Ponzu Sauce

1. Whisk the garlic, scallions, soy sauce, rice vinegar, lemon juice, and salt and pepper to taste in a medium bowl until blended.

Steps to Sear the Albacore

2. Preheat a medium-sized skillet. Be sure it's nice and hot. To test, flick water in the skillet; if it sizzles and evaporates right away, the pan is hot.

3. Sear the albacore for about 3 minutes on each side. You want the albacore to be cooked on the outside but still nice and pinkish red on the inside.

4. Dip the seared albacore right into the Ponzu sauce and put on platter in the fridge for about 5 minutes, until the albacore is cool.

5. Cut the cooled albacore lengthwise into ½-inch strips. Then put the strips back into the Ponzu sauce and marinate for at least another 5 minutes, but no more than 30 minutes, before serving.

Serves 2

Firecracker Shrimp

The longer you soak the shrimp in the hot sauce, the spicier they will be. Cook with the shell on or off. The important part is to have them deveined, unless you like eating shrimp waste. Remember, if you don't peel them before cooking, you have to peel them before putting them in your mouth — if you are impatient, like me, you'll want to do it beforehand so you can eat more quickly.

Ingredients

1 pound medium to large shrimp, deveined (see page 109)

½ bottle Frank's Red Hot Sauce

1 "eyedropper" Quaker Steak and Lube Atomic Wing Sauce

(you can use less hot sauce or none at all — just call them Wimp Shrimp)

Salt and freshly ground black pepper

1 tablespoon butter

The Steps

1. Mix the shrimp, Frank's Red Hot Sauce, Atomic Wing Sauce, and salt and pepper to taste in a large bowl. Marinate for 30 minutes in the fridge.

2. Melt the butter in a large skillet over medium heat; make sure it does not burn.

3. Sauté the shrimp for 7 to 10 minutes, or until they are pink and cooked through.

4. Grab a bunch of paper towels, 'cause it's going to be messy.

Serves 2

Crab-Stuffed Avocado

A great appetizer or light meal if you are going the fish route for dinner. Be careful taking the skin off the avocado. You want to leave it looking like an avocado.

Ingredients

1 avocado, halved, peeled, and pitted

Juice of ½ medium-sized lemon (about 1½ tablespoons)

1 can (8 ounces) crab-meat, drained and flaked apart

1 tablespoon mayonnaise

Salt and freshly ground black pepper

1 tomato, cut into chunks

1 tablespoon creamy Caesar dressing

The Steps

1. Put the avocado halves on a plate. Squeeze the lemon juice on both. (This prevents them from turning brown.)

2. Mix the crabmeat, mayonnaise, and salt and pepper to taste in a bowl.

3. Stuff the mixture into each half of the avocado until it overflows.

4. Mix the tomato and dressing in another bowl and serve as a garnish.

Serves 2

Serving with Style

✳ Serve on a bed of crisp iceberg or Boston lettuce.

✳ Lay the avocado halves in a pool of Caesar dressing and then stuff with crab

✳ Arrange the tomato and dressing on the plate, slice the avocado and fan it out in the middle, and serve with a scoop of crab salad on the side.

Pan-Fried Sole

Sole is a thin white fish that packs a lot of flavor. There are all kinds of different soles and they will all work with this recipe. Petrale and Dover sole are the best but also the most expensive. Sole is actually a variety of flounder, so other fish in the flounder family — plaice, for example — make an excellent substitute.

Ingredients

1 pound sole fillets

Salt and freshly
ground black
pepper

1 cup flour

1 large egg

1 tablespoon water

1 cup bread crumbs

4 tablespoons
(½ stick) butter

1 lemon, cut in half
for squeezing

2 tablespoons
parsley, minced

The Steps

1. Heat a large skillet over medium heat. Be sure it is nice and hot.

2. Pat dry both sides of the fish with a paper towel. (This allows the bread crumbs to stick better to the fish.) Season with the salt and pepper to taste.

3. Spread the flour on a plate.

4. Beat the egg and water in a bowl until smooth.

5. Spread the bread crumbs on another plate.

6. Melt the butter, but don't let it burn.

7. Lay both sides of each fillet in the flour, then the egg wash, then cover completely with the bread crumbs.

8. Lay the fillets in the pan. They should sizzle. Cook until golden brown, 5 to 7 minutes on each side.

9. Set the fillets on a plate, squeeze the lemon over them, and sprinkle with the parsley.

Serves 2

✳ To test doneness of fish, follow instructions on page 97.

Sea Bass with 3 Citrus Sauce

If you can't get sea bass, any firm white fish, like halibut, snapper, or monkfish, will work. The chile is optional but it gives the fish a spicy, citrus taste.

Ingredients

¼ cup orange juice
(freshly squeezed is a nice touch but from a carton does the trick as well)

Juice of 1 medium-sized lime (about 2 tablespoons)

Juice of ⅔ medium-sized lemon (about 2 tablespoons)

2–5 cloves garlic, minced

1 tablespoon honey

Salt and freshly ground black pepper

1 chile of your choice (if desired)

1–2 pounds sea bass

OPTION 1

Grill

The Steps

1. If baking, preheat the oven to 350°F. If broiling, preheat the broiler before the marinated fish is ready. If grilling, see page 99 for preheating instructions.

2. Mix the orange juice, lime juice, lemon juice, garlic, honey, salt and pepper to taste, and (if desired) the chile in a large bowl.

3. Add the sea bass to the mixture, making sure it is completely submerged, and marinate for no more than 10 minutes. If you marinate for too long, the acid from the citrus will actually start to cook the fish and the fish will fall apart.

Grill Option
Grill the marinated fish for about 5 minutes on each side, or until it is hot and flakes nicely.

Bake Option
Bake the marinated fish at 350°F for 15 to 20 minutes, or until flaky.

Broil Option
Broil the marinated fish for 7 to 10 minutes, or until flaky.

Serves 2 or 3

OPTION 2
Bake

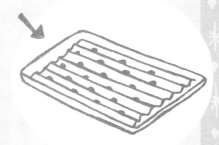

OPTION 3
Broil

Skewered Scallops

Scallops are easy and they make a great meal with pasta or rice.

Ingredients

2 shallots, chopped

4 tablespoons white wine

2 tablespoons olive oil

2 tablespoon parsley, finely chopped

Salt and freshly ground black pepper

1 pound medium to large sea scallops

The Steps

1. Preheat the broiler.

2. Whisk the shallots, wine, oil, 1 tablespoon of the parsley, and salt and pepper to taste in a large bowl until well blended.

3. Add the scallops and stir so they are completely coated. Let them sit for about 2 minutes.

4. Skewer the marinated scallops and arrange on a baking sheet if one will fit under your broiler. If not, line the broiler with foil. Broil the skewers for about 8 minutes, until scallops are firm and white all the way through. Continually check and turn them while broiling.

5. Slide the scallops off the skewers and sprinkle with the remaining parsley and any juices that collected on the foil.

Serves 2 or 3

Serving It Up
Serve scallops on their own or over pasta or rice with fresh diced tomatoes and chopped herbs. If you plan to grill, include mushrooms, onions, and red peppers on your skewers.

Chapter 8

Date Recipes

When it's time to show off a little and impress that special date, these recipes will help you in your quest. They are a little more complex, but look at it this way — you could be cooking for the person you end up spending the rest of your life with. Or at least the next few weeks. You can accompany these dishes with any of my salads from chapter 4 or vegetables from chapter 5. Roasted potatoes will work, too. The most important thing to remember is to relax; you are in control of the food, and it will taste good.

Pistachio-Crusted Halibut

*I was in Arizona on a hot date, and we ordered this dish
at a restaurant. We had such a great time and the food was
so excellent I thought this would be a great meal for someone else
on a special date. When I asked for the recipe, the chef told me,
"That's my little secret." Here's my interpretation of this wonderful
dish — it's not a secret and it's just as delicious!*

The Steps

1. Preheat the oven to 400°F.

2. Put the crushed pistachios in a bowl.

3. Put the egg and salt and pepper in another bowl.

4. Dunk the halibut in the egg, then coat well with the pistachios.

5. Melt the butter in a large, ovenproof skillet.

6. Cook the halibut in the butter for 2 minutes on each side. This seals the pistachios and flavor.

7. Move the skillet to the oven and bake for 15 to 20 minutes, or until fish flakes easily when tested with a fork.

Serves 2

Ingredients

½ pound pistachios, shelled and crushed

1 egg, beaten until smooth

Salt and freshly ground black pepper

2 pieces halibut, 6–8 ounces each

1 tablespoon butter

Crushing Nuts

Crush the pistachios by placing them on a cutting board under a clean, dry dish towel and gently hitting it all over with a hammer or mallet. You can also use a rolling pin or a heavy wooden spoon. **Be careful not to hit too hard or apply too much pressure, or you will make a nut paste**.

You can also chop the nuts with a large chef's knife. Watch your fingers, though, and be careful because the nuts will want to slide all over the counter.

Prepping a Dinner Date #1

Preplanning is vital. Open the wine so it can breathe. This brings out the natural bouquet of the wine (it really does, and besides, it makes you look like you know what you are doing). You can never go wrong with candles — they are romantic (duh), and candlelight can hide almost any cooking mistake as well as a destroyed kitchen. Stick some flowers in a vase, and a nice clean tablecloth is always good. Whatever you do, DO NOT use paper towels as napkins. Find some cloth napkins from a friend or family member. Nothing is cheesier than a great dinner and cheap napkins.

Lemon Caper Butter Fish

Use any firm, white-fleshed fish for this recipe. I like orange roughy or red snapper. Sole is very tasty too.

Ingredients

2 fish fillets,
6–8 ounces each

Salt and freshly
ground black
pepper

1 tablespoon butter

½ teaspoon
olive oil

Juice of ⅔ medium-
sized lemon (about
2 tablespoons)

1 small (4-ounce)
jar capers, drained

2 lemon wedges,
for garnish

1 tablespoon
chopped fresh
parsley, for garnish

The Steps

1. Season both sides of the fish fillets with the salt and pepper to taste.

2. Melt the butter and oil in a large skillet over medium-high heat.

3. Add the fish, lemon juice, and capers to the skillet. Cook for 5 to 7 minutes on each side, or until the fish flakes easily when tested with a fork.

4. Garnish with the lemon wedges and parsley.

Serves 2

Serving It Up

The lemon wedges and parsley are a very important part of the presentation of this meal. Use the nicest plates you have. If you use paper plates, don't expect a second date. You should serve the fish immediately, so prepare your salad or side dish beforehand. Rosemary Roasted Red Potatoes (page 20) or Roasted Asparagus (page 76) are delicious with this. My 50/50 Artichokes (page 80) are good too.

Whitefish vs. White Fish

Whitefish is an actual fish. It's a freshwater fish related to salmon. The flesh is firm and white and higher in fat.

Orange roughy is a firm, white-fleshed fish (a white fish, not whitefish) with a low fat content and mild flavor.

Real sole is from Europe, so you will only find it frozen here, and it is pretty expensive — this is usually what **Dover sole** refers to. BUT in this country the fish called **flounder or petrale sole** (which is the same thing) is usually cheaper.

Bluefish, Redfish, Goldfish

Now, bluefish is actually blue, or at least a dark, silvery gray color. This is because of how much work it does — it's actually called the **bulldog of the sea.** The meat of bluefish is very oily and fishy but it is still great to grill or broil and can be combined with other strong flavors because that of the fish is so assertive.

Red snapper is a reddish pink color and very lean and firm.

You can't eat your goldfish but there are some very tasty little silvery fish that you can eat. **Sardines, anchovies, herring,** and **mackerel** all can be grilled or fried or, more commonly, cured and packed in oil.

Sexy Citrus Scallops

Here's the trick. Marinate the scallops in citrus juice for just 5 minutes or less. They're like sponges, and they'll get mushy if allowed to marinate longer. You and, more important, your date will be bummed. Try my Asian Cucumber Salad (page 68) with this dish.

Ingredients

½ cup low-sodium soy sauce

4 tablespoons fresh lemon juice

4 tablespoons fresh lime juice

1 teaspoon sugar

1 quarter-sized piece of fresh ginger, skinned and chopped fine

Freshly ground black pepper

1½ pounds large sea scallops

1 tablespoon olive oil

2 lemon wedges

Secret Ingredient

1 tablespoon toasted sesame seeds

Tip

You will be using your hands. Make sure you wash them. I grab a small towel and stick it in my front pocket and use it for wiping and drying my hands. Otherwise, you will go through 50 paper towels.

The Steps

1. Mix the soy sauce, lemon juice, lime juice, sugar, ginger, and pepper to taste in a large bowl.

2. Add the scallops to the bowl and gently move them around to coat. Allow them to marinate NO MORE than 5 minutes.

3. Heat the oil in a large skillet.

4. Drain the liquid off the scallops, making sure they are not dripping with marinade.

5. Sauté the scallops for 2 to 3 minutes on each flat side, or until golden brown.

6. Put the scallops on two plates, sprinkle with the toasted sesame seeds, and garnish with the lemon wedges. Enjoy your date.

Serves 2

The Toasted Seed

Put sesame seeds on a small piece of aluminum foil and bake on high (about 400°F, or broil, in most toaster ovens), in the toaster oven until they are dark brown. It takes only a few minutes, so keep an eye on them. This gives the scallops a delicious taste and crunchy texture.

The Munchies Tool Box

Your toaster oven is one of the most important kitchen tools you own, second in usefulness only to the microwave. You just can't live the Munchie life without one. That said, it's important to know what your toaster can and cannot do. It can make toast; it cannot make bread. It can warm up leftovers; it cannot roast loins of pork. You can make mini muffins and cookies in it (some toaster ovens even come with little muffin pans), but you probably should not try to bake a cake in it. The greatest thing about your toaster oven is that it is fast. It warms up fast and cools down fast. This is perfect when you want to avoid preheating the oven.

Prepping a Dinner Date #2

Whatever you do, don't forget about the food! One time I got caught up conversing about what a great time I was having, and all of a sudden there was smoke everywhere. While I got a great sympathy laugh out of my date, the landlord was not too happy, and cleaning it all up really sucked. So keep checking on the food. While you're in the kitchen, you will have time to think of more great stories and funnies to impress the one you're cooking for.

Baked Pork Loin

Serve with red wine and your favorite salad, I love this dish with a baked casserole like my Mushroom & Potato au Gratin (page 88).

Ingredients

2 cuts pork loin, 1 pound each

2 tablespoons (¼ stick) butter

5 sprigs fresh rosemary or 1 tablespoon dried

(if you use dried rosemary, you should crush it and rub the meat with it before searing)

5 cloves garlic, chopped

Salt and freshly ground black pepper

The Steps

1. Preheat the oven to 350°F.

2. Sear the pork loins with the butter, rosemary, garlic, and salt and pepper to taste for 3 minutes on both sides in an ovenproof skillet over high heat.

3. Put the skillet in the oven and bake, uncovered, for 20 to 30 minutes, or until the meat is white and cooked through.

4. Remove from the heat. Let the skillet sit for 5 minutes to seal in the juices.

5. Cut the pork loins into 1- to 2-inch slices and serve.

Serves 2

Marinate Your Meat Options

Pour your favorite dark beer or about 1½ cups of red wine into a medium-sized bowl, along with the rosemary, salt, and pepper, to cover the meat (add more beer, wine, or water if the meat isn't covered). Allow it to sit for at least 1 hour and up to 4 hours in the refrigerator. Drain the liquid and let any excess liquid drip off. Place in skillet and carry on from step 3.

Roasting Garlic

When you roast garlic, not only does it develop a totally delicious melt-in-your mouth flavor without the sharp garlicky taste you associate with bad breath; it also changes in consistency, easing the peeling process. And no chopping!

Preheat the oven to 400°F. Cut off the top of a large garlic head (the top part is the end that tapers, not the end that it rests on) and peel away the outside paper. Rub the head with a little olive oil and wrap in a piece of heavy-duty aluminum foil. Stick it in the oven right on the rack and roast for about 45 minutes. When you open the foil, be careful — there will be steam.

Carefully pinch the head. The cloves should squeeze and feel soft. If not, let it roast for another 5 minutes or so. When it's done, you just squeeze the bottom and the beautiful, golden, roasted garlic gloves should pop out of the cut on top like toothpaste. It should be incredibly soft and easy to spread on anything.

Roasted Garlic Steak

I know what you're thinking: Garlic and dates don't mix. But I've served this myself with total success. As long as you both eat the garlic, you won't have to worry about your breath. The garlic has to be roasted, so give yourself an extra 45 minutes. Pick out a salad — I like the Spinach Salad with Bacon (page 58). Or try Baked Garlic Fries (page 86).

Ingredients

2 steaks,
1 pound each,
any cut you like

2 tablespoons
McCormick's Grill
Mates seasoning
blend

1 tablespoon butter

1 full bulb of garlic,
roasted

(see Roasting Garlic,
opposite page)

The Steps

1. Preheat the oven to 400°F.

2. Rub the steaks with the seasoning blend.

3. Melt the butter in a large ovenproof skillet. Cook the steaks over high heat for 3 minutes on each side, until browned.

4. Squeeze the roasted garlic out of the bulb and spread it on the steaks.

5. Put the skillet in the oven for about 20 minutes, or until desired doneness — cut the steak after 15 minutes and if it is still too pink, cook a bit longer.

Serves 2

Baked Lamb Chops with Portobello Mushrooms

Lamb is not as popular in the States as beef is, but it is a very tender, full-flavored piece of meat. If you want to experiment a little and really impress your date, try this recipe.

Ingredients

3 tablespoons
olive oil

1 tablespoon fresh
parsley, chopped

2 teaspoons
dried oregano

5 cloves garlic,
chopped

Salt and freshly
ground black
pepper

2 portobello
mushrooms, cut
into ½-inch strips

4 lamb chops
(Lamb chops are small,
that's why they're so
tender. I even recommend
preparing 3–5 per person —
just make sure your date
isn't vegan — and increase
the seasonings as needed.)

The Steps

1. Preheat the oven to 400°F.

2. Mix the oil, parsley, oregano, garlic, and salt and pepper to taste in a medium bowl.

3. Add the mushrooms and lamb chops and coat well with the oil and herbs.

4. Bake the lamb and mushrooms in a shallow baking dish for 20 minutes, or until desired doneness. The lamb will be brown but juicy and the portobellos should be tender and release juice when sliced.

Serves 2

Option

Fresh rosemary is also great with this dish; add it to the mix instead of the oregano.

You can marinate in a red wine or a dark beer — just add ¾ of a cup to the herbs and oil and let it sit for 15 to 30 minutes. Drain the liquid and bake as instructed.

Your salad choice could be Mediterranean Salad (page 65) or Summer Pasta Salad (page 62) or just a tossed green salad.

Pie and Red

I was in a pizzeria in New York once and I overheard two very seasoned ladies ordering this. When I asked them what "pie and red" meant, one of them took a long drag off her cigarette and very politely told me to "eff-off." I figured it out anyway. So this may not be the most romantic date recipe but it works, and it's so easy you'll have lots of time to worry about the atmosphere and details.

Ingredients

1 bottle red wine

1 tablespoon olive oil

3 cloves garlic, minced

Toppings, your choice

1 large frozen cheese pizza (Di Giorno 4-Cheese is good)

1 tomato, thinly sliced

1 teaspoon dried basil or handful of fresh leaves, torn

The Steps

1. Open the wine and drink a glass or two.

2. Preheat the oven to 450°F or follow the directions on the pizza box.

3. Heat the oil in a small skillet and sauté the garlic and your choice of toppings, if using, for 2 to 3 minutes, until it begins to smell good but is not yet brown.

4. Pour the mixture evenly over the pizza.

5. Lay the tomato slices on the pizza. Sprinkle the basil evenly over the tomatoes.

6. Bake until done. Follow baking time given on the package, but you may need to bake a little longer if you have added a lot of toppings.

Serves 2

The Pie Options

First of all, and I can't stress this enough, ALWAYS keep a frozen cheese pizza in your freezer. You may not know this, but the freezer was invented in order to keep pizza handy. There are so many things you can do with your frozen pizza. Here are a few of my favorites, but I guarantee that once you get the hang of things, you will be coming up with your own ideas.

✳ Add other types of cheeses: Go gourmet with goat cheese or blue, or just add extra Parmesan.

✳ Add meat: sausages, pepperoni, salami, prosciutto. Anchovies are not for the faint of heart but if you dare . . .

✳ Add other types of vegetables: Mushrooms are killer and are perfect sautéed with garlic. You can add fresh veggies or sauté them first, depending on how quickly you need to eat this pizza.

✳ Other jazzy toppings in this field are capers, jalapeños, black or green olives, pepperoncini or other marinated pepper, artichoke hearts, roasted peppers, sun-dried tomatoes, marinated mushrooms — you get the picture. Almost anything that comes in a jar works on a pizza.

Prepping a Dinner Date #3

Cooking a delicious dinner for a date is hands-down one of the most impressive feats imaginable; if you do it right and it doesn't win her or him over the person probably isn't worth dating anyway.

One great way to impress your date is to ask ahead of time what kind of mood she or he is in, fish or steak? Red wine or white? Women and men alike will think you automatically care about how they feel, and that will always get you extra brownie points.

✳ If it's warm out, you'll want to go with something light and refreshing.

✳ If it's cold out, go with something warm and filling.

✳ Cook something that you know you can do. Maybe even something you have cooked before.

✳ Read through the recipe before you start cooking, preferably the day before you start, so you have time to make sure all the ingredients are available.

✳ Cooking for a date is when all the details count, like setting a table and serving wine, salad, and bread, so think ahead and decide on everything that you want to present — not just the main dish — and how you want to present it. You definitely want to use plates, forks, and knives.

✳ Make sure you have the kitchen to yourself. Cooking for a date is not a good time for your roommate, if you have one, to start watching television in his/her underwear.

✳ Remember, confidence is a big turn-on, so cook with it and even your screwups will be okay.

✳ You can rescue any meal, and almost any date, with dessert. Make sure you have an emergency carton of ice cream and serve it with coffee, or check out some of my desserts (chapter 9). All is forgiven.

Chapter 9

Desserts

All the so-called food experts (like mothers and nutritionists and those who plan school lunches) say you should eat dessert only as the final course of a meal. That's just stupid. They are completely out of touch. I like to eat dessert depending on the mood I'm in. If it's a romantic mood, I do something creative and impressive. Then the dessert becomes an aphrodisiac. If it's a bummed-out, the-world-is-a-terrible-cold-place mood, then it's a whole different kind of dessert vibe. There is a dessert here to suit any mood at any time.

Strawberries & Cool Whip

This is a ridiculously simple recipe that your significant other will appreciate. You can make it sweet and sexy with your own creative presentation. Work your magic. On the other hand, if your other has hit the curb, even better, the more for you — you're going to need it.

Ingredients

About 20 large fresh strawberries, coarsely chopped or sliced

1 teaspoon freshly squeezed lemon juice (about ¼ medium-sized lemon)

1 tub of Cool Whip

2 teaspoons honey

The Steps

1. Put the strawberries in a large bowl.

2. Add the lemon juice and stir gently.

3. Add the Cool Whip and mix thoroughly. Spoon into chilled glasses or dishes.

4. Drizzle the honey in a circular motion around the strawberries.

Serves 2 (or 1 depressed midnight snacker)

To make this dessert a little more glamorous, in a tall glass alternately layer the strawberry slices with layers of Cool Whip. **This is only cool if you use a glass, obviously.** A champagne flute is particularly romantic and a martini glass just looks classy no matter what you put in it.

✳ Try drizzling chocolate syrup instead of honey, or, if you are trying to please a health nut, sprinkle with granola or chopped nuts.

✳ You can make this great little dessert with any fresh fruit, including peach slices, blueberries, raspberries, kiwi, mango … you get the idea.

Frozen Bananas & Chocolate

My friend Michelle Moffett came up with this simple and cool recipe. You can also do this with strawberries or butterscotch chips.

The Steps

1. Melt the chocolate in a pot over low heat, stirring constantly, or in the microwave.

2. Dip the banana rounds in the chocolate with a fork.

3. Put the coated bananas on a sheet of wax paper so they won't stick to the counter or, worse, freeze to the bottom of your freezer.

4. Stick them in the freezer for 10 to 15 minutes, or until the chocolate is nice and frozen. These are delicious on top of ice cream, too.

Ingredients

12 ounces chocolate or butterscotch chips

2 bananas, sliced into ½-inch rounds

Cherry Chocolate Ice Cream & Bailey's

Ben & Jerry's Cherry Garcia is absolutely my favorite ice cream in the world. I'm not even a Dead head. You just can't beat chocolate and cherries. Here is my twist on the scrumptious stuff; of course, you could just get the real thing and add the liqueur, but this way you control the crucial chocolate-to-cherry ratio, which in this case is lots of each.

The Steps

1. Scoop the ice cream into two bowls.

2. Sprinkle each with half the chocolate chips and cherries.

3. Pour the liqueur over the top.

Serves 2

Ingredients

1 pint very high-quality vanilla ice cream

½ cup chocolate chips or broken dark chocolate

½ cup fresh pitted cherries or frozen

(stay away from canned cherries; they are all syrupy and weird)

2 tablespoons brandy liqueur, Bailey's, or cognac

Balsamic Hawaiian Fruit

Here is a perfectly refreshing and healthy dessert you can enjoy any time of day or night. Mango is not the easiest fruit to cut, so do your best. This is tasty as a summer dessert or with my Hawaiian or Ponzu Chicken (see pages 48 and 101).

Ingredients

1 cup balsamic
vinegar

3 tablespoons
brown sugar

1–2 mangos,
peeled and cut the
best you can

1 papaya, cut
into cubes

½ pineapple,
cut into cubes

The Steps

1. Combine the balsamic vinegar and brown sugar in a small saucepan; stir constantly over medium heat until the sugar is dissolved and the consistency is syrupy like molasses, 5 to 8 minutes. Remove from the heat and allow to cool for several minutes.

2. Arrange the fruit in a bowl and drizzle with cooled syrup, lightly tossing to make sure it is well coated. Eat immediately or chill and serve with your favorite chicken dish.

Serves 1 or 2

Baked Apples & Cinnamon

This is kind of like an apple pie but without the complicated crust. It's like eating just the filling. Granny Smith and Golden Delicious apples are the best.

The Steps

1. Preheat oven to 350°F and grease a large baking dish.

2. Bring the water, apples, flour, cinnamon, sugar, butter, and vanilla to a boil in a medium-sized pot.

3. Mix well and cook at a low boil for 5 minutes. You can add more water if it seems too dry.

4. Put the apple mixture into the baking pan, sprinkle the brown sugar over it, and bake for 20 minutes. The apples should be completely tender and just starting to crisp on the edges.

Ingredients

½ cup water (more as needed)

6 apples, peeled and quartered

2 tablespoons flour

1 tablespoon ground cinnamon

1 tablespoon white sugar

1 tablespoon butter

1 teaspoon vanilla extract

1 tablespoon brown sugar

Serves 2

Serving It Up

Serve warm over vanilla, caramel, or maple ice cream, or with whipped cream. If you can't wait, just eat it hot out of the oven with a little cream over the warm apples. Baked apples are also good cold, and they can be saved for several days in the fridge and reheated. Try them over pound cake with ice cream as a full-blown dessert. Or just eat like applesauce.

Nanny's Homemade Applesauce

My Nanny, Opal Roberts, makes this all the time, so you know it's totally authentic. It's so simple that you'll never buy store-bought applesauce again. You can make big batches because it lasts for weeks and freezes really well.

Ingredients

1 cup water

10 Granny Smith or Golden Delicious apples, peeled and cored, thinly sliced, about 2½ cups

¾ cup sugar

2 tablespoons cinnamon, plus more to taste

Secret Ingredient

½ teaspoon vanilla

The Steps

1. Bring the water to a boil in a large, heavy-bottomed pot.

2. Add the apples, sugar, and cinnamon and cook over medium-low heat for 30 minutes.

3. When the apples are done, they will be very soft and easy to mush. Pour them into a large bowl. Add the vanilla and mash everything together.

4. Stick the applesauce in the fridge for at least an hour, unless you like your applesauce warm, in which case just start eating.

5. If you are at all like me, you will want to add more cinnamon.

Makes about 8 cups

White Chocolate S'mores

This recipe is ideal for camping or as a dessert at a party with a bonfire or charcoal grill. If you are stuck at home, I guess you could try using a candle ... Don't forget the skewers.

The Steps

1. Assemble the marshmallow and white chocolate on one graham cracker.

2. Use the other graham cracker to make a sandwich.

3. Eat.

Makes 1 s'more

Ingredients

2 marshmallows, toasted over a fire until browned and melted

2 whole graham crackers

1 chunk of white chocolate, about the size of a graham cracker

✻ Try using different kinds of graham crackers — chocolate and cinnamon work particularly well. Plain chocolate cookies or vanilla wafers work, as do ginger snaps. You want a fairly thin cookie that isn't too sweet on its own.

✻ Try different kinds of chocolate — dark or milk chocolate. Chocolate bars with nuts make a pretty unstable sandwich, but if you can eat it quick enough, who cares!

✻ Try using those mini Hershey bars that you get at Halloween. They work especially well with smaller cookies because the size is perfect.

Peanut Butter Cookies with Butterscotch Chips

Making cookies is not brain surgery. Just follow the instructions step by step and you'll get it. Or go to your grandparents' house and have them help you.

Ingredients

¾ cup brown sugar

¾ cup white sugar

¾ cup peanut butter, chunky or smooth

1½ sticks unsalted sweet butter at room temperature

2 large eggs

1¾ cups sifted flour

2 teaspoons baking soda

¼ teaspoon salt

½ cup butterscotch chips

The Steps

1. Preheat the oven to 350°F. Grease a large cookie sheet or use a nonstick one.

2. Combine the brown sugar, sugar, peanut butter, and butter and beat with an electric mixer. If you don't have this gadget, you can do it by hand; it just takes longer and your arm will be tired. The ingredients should be totally blended and a little fluffy.

3. Beat the eggs directly into the sugar and butter. If you are using an electric mixer, add the eggs and THEN turn on the mixer at a slow speed.

4. In a separate bowl, sift or mix together the flour, baking soda, and salt.

5. Slowly add the flour mixture to the sugar mixture — you'll need to do this by hand so the flour doesn't fly everywhere. Once the flour is incorporated, add the chips — you may need to work the dough with your hands because it will be pretty stiff.

6. Shape the dough into golf ball–sized balls with your hands and place on the prepared cookie sheet.

7. With a finger or thumb, make an indentation in the center of each cookie, flattening the ball slightly.

8. Put three butterscotch chips in the center of each cookie.

9. Bake 15 to 20 minutes, or until a light golden brown. Remove from the baking sheet and cool.

Makes 20-30 cookies, depending on how big you like them

Options

❋ Instead of butterscotch chips, mix these cookies with chocolate chips or make double-peanut cookies with peanut chips. M&M's or Reese's Pieces are a great substitute for chips.

Room Temperature Butter (don't worry; you don't need a thermometer)

This just means leave it out on the counter to soften for a couple of hours. If you forget to do that or just can't be bothered to wait so long, you can microwave it. Unwrap the sticks and cut them up into smaller chunks; they don't have to be really small, just smaller. Put in a microwave-safe bowl and heat for 20 to 30 seconds on the lowest power. To check it, mash with a fork. If it is still too hard, microwave for another 10 seconds and so on. You want it soft enough to mush up easily but not melted or completely liquid.

* Caramel butterscotch

* Fudge

* Pineapple

* Strawberry

* Marshmallow

* Double chocolate

* Maple syrup

* Honey

* Crumbled Milky Way bars

* Toasted coconut

* Cinnamon sugar, sprinkled on top

* Chopped nuts (pecans, toasted peanuts, or almonds, or try pistachios!)

* Dried cherries or apricots

* Candied dried ginger — this is out of control with vanilla ice cream and caramel syrup

Frozen Cookie Dough

I like to keep a package of cookie dough in the freezer for just about any occasion. It makes a great addition to ice-cream sundaes. Cut off a chunk and crumble or mix in.

Premade dough is also a great Munchie — use your toaster oven and follow the package instructions for baking. You can make as many as fit in your toaster or just one — your choice. Here are some different frozen cookie doughs available. Check the frozen foods section of your supermarket for other options.

* Chocolate Chip
* Oatmeal Chocolate Chip
* Peanut Butter
* Chocolate Chunk
* Sugar
* Gingerbread
* Double Chocolate Chip
* White Chocolate Chunk
* Macadamia Nut

Easy Sundaes

I once read, "Ice cream makes every day a sundae." How true! What makes these so great is that supermarkets carry all the syrups you could possibly imagine, and the toppings can be as easy or as complicated as you want.

Ingredients

2 scoops ice cream of your choice

½ cup mini marshmallows

2 tablespoons English toffee syrup

Toppings of your choice
(see Topping Options, at left)

The Steps

1. Scoop the ice cream into a bowl.

2. Sprinkle the marshmallows on the ice cream.

3. Warm the syrup in the microwave (follow instructions and times on the package) and pour over the ice cream. Add your favorite toppings.

Makes 1 portion

Serving with Style

For dark chocolate shavings, use a large bar of good chocolate — the darker, the better. Drag a vegetable peeler or a cheese slicer across the surface of the chocolate bar. (You can get tiny shavings by using a regular cheese grater.) Chocolate shavings are fantastic — they look really classy and they melt in your mouth. If you use a high-quality bar of chocolate, you will always be impressed with the results.

Brownies

Of course making packaged brownies is easy; the difficult part is choosing from your many topping options. You can make these for dessert anytime, but they are quite impressive to bring to a party.

Ingredients

1 package brownie mix

(Betty Crocker is pretty reliable but you can experiment)

Toppings of your choice

The Steps

1. Follow instructions on the brownie mix and prepare a baking pan.

2. Make the batter, following the package instructions. Mix in your favorite toppings, or sprinkle them on top once the batter is in the pan.

3. Bake as directed, or until a toothpick inserted in the middle comes out clean.

Makes one 9 x 13 pan of brownies, about 9 squares

Some of the Options

* Crushed Butterfinger or Twix bars

* M&M's — plain, peanut, or almond

* Chopped walnuts or your favorite nut

* Crushed Peanut Butter Cups

* Hershey Kisses

* Chocolate, peanut butter, or butterscotch chips

* If you stand in the candy aisle for long enough, something will come to mind . . .

Chapter 10
Party Munchies

The best way never to get invited to another party is not to bring anything. People will think your parents didn't teach you any manners. The best parties to bring something to are holiday parties, birthday parties, summer barbecues, and picnics. I promise that if you bring Munchies from this chapter, you will be on the A-list of invitees — you may even have to start a rotation schedule to keep track of the invites. So work your cooking magic and get out and meet some cool people. Remember, a stranger is just a friend you haven't met yet.

Texas Caviar Bean Dip

Texans know how to eat beans — like they're caviar!

Ingredients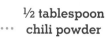

1 can (15 ounces) black beans, drained

1 can (15 ounces) black-eyed peas, drained

3 scallions, sliced thin

1 jalapeño chile, minced

2 tablespoons chopped cilantro

½ tablespoon chili powder

½ teaspoon dried oregano

½ teaspoon salt

¼ teaspoon freshly ground black pepper

Dressing

¼ cup olive oil

3 tablespoons red wine vinegar

2 cloves garlic, minced

The Steps

1. Mix the beans, peas, scallions, jalapeño, and cilantro in a large bowl.

2. To make the dressing, in a separate bowl whisk together the oil, vinegar, garlic, chili powder, oregano, salt, and pepper.

3. Pour the dressing over the bean mixture and mix well. Cover and refrigerate until ready to go.

4. Serve with chips.

Serves 5-7

The Chip: A User's Guide

Of course you have a favorite, but new chips come along every day. I like to try whatever is new but keep the old standbys handy. Here are few of my top picks, including that quintessential Munchie chip — the tortilla chip!

✱ **Mission Tortilla Chips** are the best all-around chips out there unless you get yourself to Mexico on a regular basis.

✱ **Garden of Eatin'** makes a great blue corn chip as well as a chile lime flavor.

✱ **Tostitos** restaurant-style chips, bite-size, and scoops are all good.

✱ **Ranch Doritos**

✱ **Cheetos Flamin' Hot**

✱ **Ruffles Original** are my potato chips of choice, though there are lots of tasty gourmet options out there too. Salt and vinegar is usually a winner.

✱ **Sun Chips**

✱ **Pretzels** — so technically they're not a chip, but psychologically I can't separate them. Besides, they're in the same aisle of the grocery store. I like the classic **Rold Gold** but **Newman's Own Salt and Pepper Pretzels** are pretty tasty too.

Dee's Best Salsa

I got this recipe from Danielle Galvan. I was hooked the first time she made it. It is so simple, yet big in taste. Eat with your favorite tortilla chips.

Ingredients

10–12 fresh Roma tomatoes, chopped

5 jalapeño chiles, chopped

4 or 5 scallions, chopped

1 bundle cilantro, chopped, about 1 cup

1 medium white onion, chopped

2 cloves garlic, chopped

1 teaspoon garlic salt

Salt and freshly ground black pepper

2 cans (28 ounces each) plain tomato sauce

Juice of 1 lime, (about 3 tablespoons)

The Steps

1. Mix the tomatoes, jalapeños, scallions, cilantro, onion, garlic, and salt and pepper to taste in a large bowl.

2. Add the tomato sauce and mix thoroughly.

3. Add lime juice, taste, and adjust seasonings. Let sit at room temperature for at least 10 minutes before serving so flavors fuse.

Makes about 10 cups

Coleslaw with Peanuts

This recipe comes from the Tam O' Shanter Inn — a restaurant I worked at for almost a whole day. I spilled a tray of water glasses on a woman while she was having her birthday party. No, I didn't get fired, because I ran like the wind. The inn's coleslaw is to die for and luckily I got the recipe on my way out.

Ingredients

8 cups shredded cabbage

1½ cups chopped celery

⅔ cup diced scallions (white and green parts)

½ cup chopped cocktail peanuts

⅔ cup Lawry's Italian Salad Dressing

1 teaspoon Lawry's Seasoned Salt

½ teaspoon freshly ground black pepper

The Steps

1. Lightly toss together the cabbage, celery, scallions, and peanuts in a large mixing bowl.

2. Pour the dressing over the salad. Add the seasoned salt and pepper and toss again.

3. Refrigerate for at least 20 minutes. If you can't wait, I understand. This salad will keep for a day in the fridge, but any longer and the peanuts start to get soggy.

Serves 8

Munchies Flavor Tip
Lawry's is just a blend of seasonings and salt. It also makes great salad dressings and marinades. I like to keep a couple of kinds of seasoned salt around. It's great for seasoning meats and sauces and saves the hassle of 15 different spice jars. There are tons of brands out there; experiment and find your favorite or check out my Cool Products (see page 180).

Bruschetta

I dated this girl from France who could really cook. She made this recipe all the time. I'll say there was one good thing about that relationship — the food! Here's my version of her delectable, chunky tomato toasts; they're perfect for any holiday party or as an appetizer.

Ingredients

10 Roma tomatoes, chopped

10 leaves fresh basil, rolled up and coarsely chopped

10 cloves garlic, minced

½ cup grated Parmesan

4 tablespoons olive oil

½ teaspoon salt

Freshly ground black pepper to taste

1 baguette

The Steps

1. Preheat the oven or toaster oven to 350°F.

2. Mix the tomatoes, basil, garlic, Parmesan, oil, salt, and pepper in a large bowl.

3. Put in the fridge for 10 to 30 minutes. The longer you can wait, the tastier it will be.

4. Cut the baguette into ½-inch slices and toast them on a baking sheet until they're a little crispy, so they can soak up all the juices of the tomato sauce without getting too soggy.

5. Arrange the toasted baguette slices on a plate and spoon some of the tomato mixture onto each one. Pile it high and eat carefully.

Serves 5-10, depending on how many slices you get out of the baguette

The Bruschetta Options

✱ Toast the baguette slices with a little grated Parmesan on top.

✱ Garnish the bruschetta with slices of black olives or capers.

✱ Crumble a little bit of goat cheese or other gourmet cheese on top of the tomato or on the slices of bread before you toast them.

✱ Dribble a little balsamic vinegar over the tomatoes on each slice.

Bucky's Secret Sangría

Friends call me before parties and ask if I'm bringing this secret sauce. Remember, kids, if you're under 21, you can't make this with wine, but if you're 26 and still in college, well, that's another story.

Ingredients

4 bottles (750 ml) of inexpensive red wine

1 cup sugar

Juice of 5 medium-sized oranges (2–2½ cups)

Juice of 2 medium-sized lemons (about 6 tablespoons)

Juice of 2 medium-sized limes (about 4 tablespoons)

1 green apple, cored and sliced thin

Secret Ingredient

2 cups of brandy
(this is what gets everyone fired up)

The Steps

1. You will need a big container or punch bowl for this recipe.

2. Mix the wine and sugar in the largest pot you have; stir well until the sugar dissolves.

3. Add the orange, lemon, and lime juices.

4. Allow the apple slices to float on top of the sangría for decoration (they suck up the sangría, so I always eat them, too).

5. Add the brandy and mix well. Cover and refrigerate for as long as you can.

6. Serve with ice in the glasses (NOT in the bowl, or the sangría will get too diluted).

Serves 8-10

Guacamole

You can keep it chunky or blend until creamy. If you like it spicy, add your favorite hot sauce.

Ingredients

8 ripe avocados, peeled and pitted

Juice of 1 lemon (about 3 tablespoons)

1 teaspoon salt

1 large bag of your favorite tortilla chips

The Steps

1. Place the avocado, lemon juice, and salt in a large bowl and mash with the back of a large spoon or a fork until you have the desired consistency.

2. Add extra ingredients of choice (see box) and stir in gently. Refrigerate for 30 minutes.

3. Serve with the tortilla chips.

Serves 12

The Extra Options
1 tablespoon of Parmesan cheese OR diced tomatoes (cherry tomatoes have less water and hold together best) OR minced sweet white onion or red onion. Try lime juice instead of lemon or add a tablespoon of balsamic vinegar. Mix in some chopped cilantro or a jalapeño or other hot chile, or just add a few drops of your preferred hot sauce. Tabasco works well. When you are adding stuff, start out with a little and keep tasting it. Gradually add more until it tastes just right.

Crab-Stuffed Deviled Eggs

You can never go wrong with this at a party. Just wait for the reaction when people find out there is real crab in them.

Ingredients

12 jumbo or extra-large hard-cooked eggs

2 cans (6 ounces each) crabmeat, drained and flaked

½ cup mayonnaise

½ teaspoon ground cumin

½ teaspoon paprika

4 drops Worcestershire sauce or to taste

1 teaspoon freshly ground black pepper, to taste

½ teaspoon salt

1 can (10 ounces) black olives, sliced in half, for garnish

The Steps

1. When the eggs are cool enough to handle, remove the shells and cut the eggs in half lengthwise. Carefully remove the yolks while keeping the egg white halves intact. Set the whites aside.

2. Mash the yolks in a bowl until smooth. Stir in the crabmeat, mayonnaise, cumin, paprika, Worcestershire sauce, pepper, and salt. Make sure all the ingredients are well blended.

3. Fill each egg white half with the mixture. You should have enough to slightly overstuff them all.

4. Garnish with ½ olive on top of each egg and an extra sprinkle of paprika, if you like.

Makes 1 dozen deviled eggs or 2 dozen halves

How to Hard-Cook an Egg

Place eggs in a medium-sized saucepan and fill it with enough water to cover them. Bring to a fast boil and then turn off the heat. Let the eggs sit, covered, for 15 to 20 minutes, depending on their size. Drain the water and rinse the eggs under cold water to stop the cooking and make them easier to peel.

When cool enough to handle, crack the eggs all over by gently tapping or rolling against a counter top. You should be able to peel easily. Hard-cooked eggs can be kept for 4 days in their shells in the fridge. It is easier to use hard-cooked eggs that are completely cool.

Roasted Balls

I came up with this recipe after another horrific round of golf. Which, I will say, I am officially retired from, but not by choice. I'm retired because I've thrown all of my clubs into the lake outta frustration. I know, I know, patience is a virtue. Or golf is just too hard! (You can also use these in meatball sandwiches.)

Ingredients

1 pound ground turkey or beef

2 egg yolks

¼ cup chopped parsley

2 tablespoons grated Parmesan

2–5 cloves garlic, minced

1 small onion, finely diced

1 teaspoon cayenne pepper or chili powder

Salt and freshly ground black pepper to taste

The Steps

1. Preheat the oven to 400°F. Line a large baking sheet with aluminum foil.

2. Mix together all of the ingredients in a large mixing bowl, using your hands!

3. Mold the mixture into golf ball–sized meatballs.

4. Bake the meatballs on the prepared baking sheet until they are hot in the center, about 20 minutes.

Serves 6

Serving Roasted Balls

If you are bringing the balls to a party, make them the night before and refrigerate.

Bring them cold; they can be reheated quickly in a microwave. If you are serving them at home, keep them warm in the oven on low heat, covered. They can warm for about an hour without drying out. Serve on a large plate with toothpicks and a little marinara sauce or hot sauce for dipping.

Other Stuff You Can Do with Roasted Balls

Use the balls for **meatball subs or sandwiches** or in any spaghetti sauce. Just add them to plain red sauce and heat in a skillet, then serve **over pasta**. Or put them on a **toasted hero roll** or Italian bread with mozzarella and Parmesan. Or stuff them into a sub with sautéed peppers and onions. Either way, it's a hero! Or you can **try to play golf** with them — you'll get about as far as I usually did.

Cream Cheese Hot Poppers

A crunchy shell and a mild, creamy, melted cheese center make these poppers taste like they could win an award. They haven't yet but they could...

Ingredients

10 whole jalapeño chiles

8 ounces cream cheese (mashed if in stick form)

2 tablespoons flour

2 large eggs, beaten until smooth

1 teaspoon garlic powder

½ teaspoon cayenne pepper

½ teaspoon paprika

1 cup bread crumbs

The Steps

1. Preheat the oven to 400°F. Grease a baking sheet with butter or cooking spray.

2. Using a small, sharp paring knife, remove the tops of the chiles. Cut carefully so as to keep the top and stem intact. Set the tops aside. Hollow out each chile by removing the seeds and the white membranes.

3. Using a spoon or your fingers, stuff the cream cheese into each chile until it's full. Replace the chile top with stem and gently press it down to seal the cheese inside. Set aside.

4. Mix the flour, eggs, garlic powder, cayenne, and paprika until the flour is completely dissolved.

5. Put the bread crumbs in a separate bowl.

6. Carefully dunk the chiles in the egg mix, completely drenching them. Then coat with bread crumbs so they are completely covered. You might find it easier to lay the egg-soaked chiles in the bread crumbs and spoon extra crumbs over in order to coat entirely.

7. Bake the chiles on the prepared baking sheet for 20 minutes, or until peppers are tender. You will want to serve these right away, so if you are bringing them to a party, bake them for 15 minutes and then reheat for another 5 to 10 minutes once you are there.

Makes 10 poppers

Cheese Choices

You can substitute 8 ounces of shredded sharp Cheddar for the cream cheese. Or get extra spicy and use shredded Pepper Jack. Shredded mozzarella is another tasty alternative, and milder.

Stuffed Potato Skins

Each potato will give you two skins. You have to bake the potatoes first, so there's about 45 minutes of cooking time involved here. Russet potatoes work the best — make sure whatever you use is large with a thick skin. Those little new potatoes will not give you much to chew on.

Ingredients

5 russet potatoes (the bigger the potato, the bigger the skin)

10 slices of bacon

½ cup milk

2 tablespoons (¼ stick) unsalted butter

8 ounces grated Cheddar

1 scallion, finely chopped

12 ounces sour cream

1 tablespoon cayenne pepper and/or chili powder, if desired

The Steps

1. Preheat the oven to 450°F.

2. Scrub and clean the potatoes of all dirt. Pat dry with a towel.

3. Wrap each potato in aluminum foil and bake for 45 to 60 minutes, or until tender. Remove from the heat, but leave the oven on.

4. While the potatoes are baking, cook the bacon in a large skillet over medium heat for 5 minutes on each side, or until crunchy. Drain on a paper towel. Chop and set aside.

5. Cover a large baking sheet with aluminum foil.

6. When the potatoes are done and cool enough to handle, cut them in half and spoon out the insides, leaving the shell intact.

7. Put all the insides of the potatoes into a large mixing bowl.

8. Add the chopped bacon, milk, and butter. Mix until you have a smooth and creamy consistency.

9. Spoon equal amounts of the mixture into each potato skin, filling them about halfway.

10. Sprinkle with the cheese.

11. Bake the stuffed skins for 15 to 20 minutes, or until cheese is melted and the skins are crispy. Remove from the oven.

12. Sprinkle the scallions on top of each skin.

13. Mix together the sour cream and cayenne in a separate bowl. Use as a dip.

10 stuffed skins

Marinated & Roasted Pork Ribs

These are my aunt Janice's favorite, so I make them for her every Christmas. The trick is to marinate them overnight. I use spare ribs, but baby backs will work, too.

Ingredients

3 pounds pork ribs (one full slab), cut into single rib pieces
(you can do this yourself, buy precut ribs in a package, or ask your butcher to do it)

½ cup brown sugar

½ cup low-sodium soy sauce

2 tablespoons honey

1 teaspoon salt

1 teaspoon freshly ground black pepper

The Steps

1. Combine the ribs, brown sugar, soy sauce, honey, salt, and pepper in a large resealable plastic bag.

2. Shake the bag to mix well. Marinate overnight or for at least 8 hours in the refrigerator.

3. Preheat the oven to 350°F. Remove the ribs from the bag.

4. Sauté the ribs in a large skillet for 5 minutes. This will fuse the flavor in the ribs before baking.

5. Bake the sautéed ribs in a baking dish for 15 minutes, uncovered. Because ribs are small and there is not a lot of meat on them, check the oven after 10 minutes and keep checking until done, making sure they do not burn. They should be browned and completely hot throughout. If you're afraid they're cooking too fast and starting to burn, cover the dish with aluminum foil or a lid and continue cooking.

Serves 5-7

Chapter 11

Late-Night Bites

Late-night bites are necessary when you're busy all day, get home late, and don't want to cook a so-called meal. Or you're awake for no reason at 3:00 A.M., staggering toward the fridge in the dark. You open the door and there's a blinding light. After fighting off the initial shock and adjusting your eyes, you're ready to try some of these quick and bare recipes. I've designed most to feed only one person because when the late-night munchies strike, you're usually on your own.

The Official Munchies International Refrigerator Door

It seems that every culture has its own versions of ketchup, mustard, and mayo. Those condiments that every refrigerator door, no matter how empty and unused, has. Using condiments from other countries and cuisines is a fantastic, inexpensive way to develop new tastes, improve on boring basics, and try out all kinds of cool and creative flavors. So don't avoid the international aisle!

❋ **Capers:** pickled in vinegar and great with seafood, eggs, and on pizzas.

❋ **Kimchee or Kimchi:** a type of pickled Korean cabbage.

❋ **Pepperoncini:** pickled, medium-hot peppers.

❋ **Marinated roasted peppers:** another scrumptious sandwich item or pizza topper.

❋ **Mango or lime pickle:** an Indian pickle used as a condiment.

❋ **Chutney:** a sweet-and-sour relish perfect on cheese sandwiches and cheeseburgers. Use it like ketchup.

❋ **Colman's Hot Mustard** is so good with sausages and mac & cheese.

❋ **Wasabi and pickled ginger:** two Japanese condiments for seafood and in marinades. Add some wasabi to mayo for a kick; it's great on burgers.

❋ **Hoy Fung Sriracha Garlic Hot Sauce:** one of my favorites; chilies, garlic, and vinegar, a great all-around flavoring.

❋ **Nutella:** an addictive chocolate hazelnut spread that can be used on toast, cookies, or peanut butter sandwiches.

❋ **Pesto, oil-packed sun-dried tomatoes, roasted peppers:** sandwich spreads and pizza enhancers.

❋ **Pickled onions, stuffed olives:** not just for cocktails, these are perfect on pizzas and in sandwiches and salads.

❋ **Marinated/pickled Italian-style vegetables:** a delicious condiment or an addition to salads or sandwiches.

❋ **Mexican condiments:** include anything from Ortega, Las Palmas sauces, La Victoria salsas, Tapitio and Cholula hot sauce, and that standard Pace Picanté.

Eggo Ice-Cream Sandwiches

Warm, crunchy Eggos go great with ice cream. If you want, you can warm up the syrup when you pour it on top, the ice cream will melt quicker, so eat up!

Ingredients

2 Eggo waffles

1 scoop vanilla ice cream

2 tablespoons maple syrup

Options

* Chocolate syrup
* Jam
* Nutella
* Cool Whip
* Honey and peanut butter
* Hot fudge sauce
* Fresh or frozen fruit
* Ben & Jerry's Cherry Garcia ice cream

The Steps

1. Toast your Eggos.

2. Put a scoop of ice cream on one Eggo, then top with the other Eggo.

3. Drench with maple syrup or topping of your choice.

Serves 1

Mini Tostadas

My version of the regular-sized tostada, but a lot easier to make. It's too much trouble to make that big flaky shell you see in restaurants. Trust me, I found out the hard way, and besides, you need a deep fryer. So I came up with these bite-sized treats.

Ingredients

10–20 round tortilla chips

1 can (14 ounces) refried beans

1 cup leftover ground beef, steak
or whatever meat you have — make sure it's cooked

½ cup shredded cheese, any kind

Dash hot sauce for each chip
(see Hot Sauce List, page 47)

Options

Sour cream, guacamole, salsa, jalapeños

The Steps

1. Heat the oven or toaster oven to 350°F.

2. Select 20 or so chips that are fairly flat and unbroken and lay them out on a piece of aluminum foil.

3. Spread a layer of the beans evenly over each chip.

4. Add the beef, cheese, and hot sauce in layers.

5. Bake for 5 minutes, or until the cheese is melted and everything is hot.

6. Top with sour cream, guacamole, salsa, or jalapeños.

Serves 1

Mexican Tuna Wrap

My buddy and I used to eat these when we came home after a night of partying. Totally filling and surprisingly healthy.

The Steps

1. Mix the tuna, mayonnaise, mustard, and salt and pepper to taste in a bowl.

2. Warm the tortilla directly on a stovetop burner over medium heat, flipping frequently so it doesn't burn. This should take only a couple of minutes. Alternatively, you can warm it for a minute in the toaster oven.

3. Spoon the tuna mixture onto the middle of the warm tortilla, wrap, and eat.

Serves 1

Ingredients

1 can (6 ounces) tuna, coarsely chopped

1 tablespoon mayonnaise

½ teaspoon mustard

Salt and freshly ground black pepper

1 large flour or whole wheat tortilla

Munchie Wrap-Up Options

Depending on the state of your refrigerator at 2 A.M. (and your state of mind), there are lots of things you can add to this wrap. Here are a few I've added to my Mexican Tuna Wrap on a late-night quest for some sleep-inducing carbs and protein.

* peppers
* onions
* celery
* carrots
* cheese
* pickles
* hot chiles
* capers
* salsa
* lettuce
* tomato

Poor-Man's Pizza

Late one night while craving pizza, I realized no one was going to deliver anything to me. I looked in the fridge, found something, and came up with this. If nothing else it frees up valuable fridge space.

Ingredients

4 tablespoons tomato sauce

1 bagel or English muffin, cut in half
(any kind except raisin or blueberry)

4 tablespoons shredded cheese, any kind

Finely chopped leftover meat and/or veggies
(whatever and however much you have in the fridge)

The Steps

1. Preheat the oven or toaster oven to 400°F.

2. Spread tomato sauce over the bagel halves and sprinkle with cheese.

3. Sprinkle with whatever meat or veggies you've found in the fridge.

4. Bake for 10 minutes, or until the cheese has melted and the bagel is crispy.

Serves 1

Toppings

This pizza is the reason that the door of your refrigerator and those weird compartments at the bottom exist — find something in there and put it on top.

* Pepperoni
* Salami or sausage
* Lunch meat — ham, beef, or turkey, cut up
* Olives
* Onions
* Garlic
* Hot peppers
* Artichoke hearts

Triple Decker PB & J with Banana & Honey

I know for a fact that Jack Nicholson loves peanut butter & jelly sandwiches, so you know it's still cool to eat them. Here's my twist on the ultimate midnight Munchie.

Ingredients

3 slices bread of your choice
(I like rye, and I like it toasted.)

1 tablespoon peanut butter

1 tablespoon jelly

½ teaspoon honey

1 banana, sliced thin

The Steps

1. Lay out the bread.

2. Spread the peanut butter evenly on one slice.

3. Spread the jelly evenly on another slice.

4. Spread the honey evenly on the third slice.

5. Top the honey with the banana slices.

6. Assemble the three slices of bread to form this triple-decker delight.

Serves 1

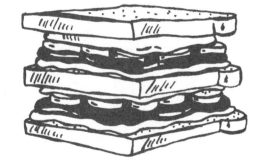

Mac & Cheese in a Box

Both Kraft and Velveeta set the standard for packaged mac & cheese back in the olden days. Now, in addition to the classic, they make all kinds of fancy flavors (everything from spirals to Alfredo sauce) that are worth checking out if you spend much time eating the stuff. You know who you are. Annie's Homegrown makes some great packaged mac & cheese and you can congratulate yourself on being healthy while eating it.

Mac & Cheese Options

✳ Mac & Cheese with Tomato: Make your mac & cheese according to the instructions on the package. When it is mixed completely, empty it into a baking dish and arrange thick slices of tomato on top. Sprinkle with extra Parmesan if you like and stick it under the broiler for 4 to 6 minutes — just enough to get it bubbling and slightly brown and crispy on top.

✳ Sprinkle the top of the mac & cheese with bread crumbs, a little butter, and extra Parmesan and broil until bubbling and crispy, about 3 minutes.

✳ Mix any of the following into the cooked mac & cheese:

✳ Halved cherry tomatoes or a few tablespoons of tomato sauce or pureé; 1 teaspoon of dried mustard powder or 1 tablespoon of hot English mustard; 1 teaspoon of cayenne pepper or paprika, chopped or crumbled bacon or diced ham, chopped fresh herbs or parsley. (Or sprinkle on top.)

✳ Experiment with different cheeses. I always add a little extra grated cheese to the dried packet. Try a sharp Cheddar, Gruyère, Parmesan, smoked Gouda, or a little crumbled blue cheese for extra flavor.

Tuna Mac & Cheese

This is really tasty when you're craving comfort food, feeling fragile, or having a flashback to school lunch. It's quick and easy to make, and it tastes amazing. I bet you'll eat the whole thing.

Ingredients

1 box macaroni & cheese

2 tablespoons milk

1 tablespoon butter

1 can (6 ounces) tuna

1 tablespoon ketchup

1 teaspoon hot sauce of your choice
(see Hot Sauce List, page 47)

¼ cup grated Cheddar or Parmesan

½ teaspoon freshly ground black pepper

Salt

The Steps

1. Follow the package directions for cooking the macaroni but DON'T follow them for the rest of the recipe. Taste the macaroni to be sure it's soft and to your liking.

2. Drain and put the macaroni in a large bowl.

3. Add the cheese packet that came in the box and the milk and butter; stir.

4. Add the tuna, ketchup, hot sauce, grated cheese, pepper, and salt to taste. Mix until the cheese is melted and well blended.

Serves 1

Quick Quesadilla

This easy recipe beats getting in your car or taking the bus and making a run for the border — or for your local all-night taco joint. It's better and cheaper, and the options are limitless.

Ingredients

1 teaspoon oil
or butter

2 corn or flour tortillas,
8 to 10 inches in
diameter

2 tablespoons refried
beans, black or pinto

2 ounces leftover
ground or chopped
meat, whatever's
in the fridge

(if it's not ground or
chopped, do so now)

1 handful chopped
veggies, whatever's
in the fridge

(if they're not chopped,
do so now)

1 handful shredded
cheese, whatever's
in the fridge

Hot sauce

(see Hot Sauce List,
page 47)

The Steps

1. Heat the oil in a large skillet over medium heat.

2. Place the tortillas on the counter.

3. Spread the beans evenly on one tortilla. Add the meat, veggies, and cheese.

4. Lay the other tortilla on top of the layered tortilla. It should look like a fat Frisbee.

5. Carefully lay the Frisbee in the skillet. Cook each side for about 5 minutes, or until the tortilla is crisp and starting to brown, the meat, veggies, and beans are hot, and the cheese is melted.

6. Remove from the skillet and cut into wedges. Douse with your favorite hot sauce.

Serves 1

The Options

✳ **Meats:** Leftover steak is your first choice, but chicken works, as do most deli meats — turkey, ham, and salami. Chop the meat and stick it in. I call for leftover meat for a reason. It must be cooked thoroughly BEFORE you add it to the quesadilla. DO NOT try this with raw hamburger!

✳ **Veggies:** These should be cooked unless you're using something soft that cooks fast, like onions, mushrooms, spinach, tomatoes, or peppers. Avoid raw carrots and broccoli — they never cook quickly enough.

✳ **Avocado** can be added on top, but don't cook it in the tortilla; it tastes better uncooked. You can also sprinkle chopped red onion or bell pepper on top.

✳ **Sour cream and salsa** are delicious on top, but I never skip the hot sauce!

11:00 P.M.
Fruit & Yogurt

You ate dinner, probably several hours ago. You may have had dessert. Now you're kind of thinking about food again and you're not going to bed anytime soon. Time for what I like to think of as my second dessert.

Take a cup or more of plain or vanilla yogurt and add your favorite fruit. Blueberries, raspberries, sliced banana, and cut-up peach are all good, but use what you have.

Try this with other flavors of yogurt, like peach or lemon. Or top it with dried fruit, chopped nuts, granola or other cereal.

11:30 P.M.
English Garlic Bread

Don't you ever crave garlic bread without the whole Italian restaurant experience? I can't think of a better late-night munchie.

Here's the trick. Toast an English muffin, and while it's toasting, sauté some garlic in about a tablespoon of butter over low heat. When the garlic starts to turn golden and smell good, drizzle the melted garlic butter over your toasted muffin. It's better than garlic knots and you don't have to order a pizza to get it. Even though it tastes like the real thing, I wouldn't try serving it to your Italian grandmother . . .

1:30 A.M.
Baked Grapefruit

If you are a normal person who is able to sleep without thinking about food, you never come up with the wild combinations of food that I do. Cinnamon and grapefruit will change how you feel about 1:30 A.M. forever.

Turn your toaster oven to 450°. Cut and section a grapefruit. Put a pat of butter in the center of each half and sprinkle with about ½ teaspoon of cinnamon and sugar. Bake the grapefruit for 10 minutes, until everything melts and you can smell the cinnamon. It helps to cover the toaster tray with foil — less mess.

2:00 A.M.
PB&L

It's two o'clock in the morning. Do you know what's in your refrigerator?

Lettuce?

I know what you're thinking — what can I do with lettuce at this point? You're thinking — he's lost his mind. I haven't, you've got to try it.

Peanut butter and lettuce is the secret weapon of the late-night snacker. Make some toast, spread with peanut butter, put lettuce on top, and munch. It's so much better than you think! If you're up for it, try topping with honey.

12:30 A.M.

Beans on Toast

This one's from my bloody friends in England. The ultimate British munchie crosses the pond surprisingly well (unlike that deep-fried Mars Bar thing which is simply depraved). Beans on Toast is a late-night staple in the UK and once you try it, you'll know why. It's another reason to keep a stash of canned beans in your kitchen. I like Bush's for the extra brown sugar and bacon. Just heat the beans on the stovetop or in the microwave and pour over toast. I know it's late, but you'll need to use a fork for this.

1:00 A.M.

Stuffed Celery

It's getting late. You just burned a bunch of calories (wink, wink) and you're craving something light but filling.

Assuming you can find some celery somewhere in your fridge (look in that bottom drawer), wash and dry the stalks and fill the tunnels with peanut butter or cream cheese. Try topping cream cheese with olives or just eat and go back to picking lint off your pajamas.

2:30 A.M.

So you liked that, did you? Want some more? It was so good you ran out of lettuce? Well, peanut butter is not one of the all-time great munchie foods for nothing. There are tons of other delicious ways of getting to the bottom of that jar. Here are a few of my faves.

* Peanut butter and banana (it was good enough for Elvis); try it grilled.
* Peanut butter and honey
* and apple slices
* and bacon on toast
* and chocolate on toast
* on frozen waffles
* on raisin bread or cinnamon toast

3:00 A.M.

Apples & Honey

Lemon is going to rescue that apple you found lingering in the back of your fridge. Slice the apple, sprinkle with lemon juice, and drizzle with honey. It won't fill you up, so you can easily head to bed after eating.

I think you should be considering that around now.

In fact — this is sort of the end of the line. I don't think I can support you scrounging for food past this hour. You need to go to bed or turn directly to chapter 1 and start making breakfast. Sweet dreams . . .

Cool Products

If your local store doesn't carry something, contact the company directly. Most of these companies will also send you free recipes for their products. I have used all of these products, so you know if they weren't cool, they wouldn't be in this cookbook. Tell them *Munchies* hooked you up.

About Pizza Website
www.aboutpizza.com

Adriana's Caravan
78 Grand Central Terminal
New York, NY 10017
www.adrianascaravan.com

Anchor Steam Brewing, Christmas Ale, Anchor Brewing Company
1705 Mariposa Street
San Francisco, CA 94107
(415) 863-8350
www.anchorbrewing.com

Atlantic Spice Co.
2 Shore Road, P.O. Box 205; North Truro, MA 02652; (800) 316-7965
www.atlanticspice.com

Arizona Gunslinger, Smokin' Hot Sauce
Mesa, AZ; (800) 359-3912
www.azgunslinger.com

Benihana Sesame Garlic Steak Sauce
Portland, OR
www.yoshidafoodsinternational.com

Detroit Spice Co.
2517 Russell Street; Detroit, MI 48207; (313) 393-7980
www.Detroitspiceco.com

E' Liza J Gourmet
1302 Cedar Hills Boulevard
Cedar Park, TX 78613-6724
(512) 260-8956
www.ELizaJFoods.com

Fiery Foods
Albuquerque, NM; (505) 873-8680
www.fiery-foods.com

Frank's Red Hot Sauce
Wayne, N.J.; (800) 888-0192
www.franksredhot.com

The Great American Spice Co.
Fort Wayne, IN; (888) 502-8058
www.americanspice.com

Grill Mates
McCormick & Company, Inc.
211 Schilling Circle; Hunt Valley, MD 21031; (800) 632-5847

Hickins Farms
Dummerston, VT; (802) 254-2146

Iron Q
82 Campbell Avenue; West Haven, CT 06516; www.ironq.com

Jack Daniels Grilling Sauce
Pittsburgh, PA; (800) 577-2823

Kona Coast Smoky Barbecue Sauce
G.L. Mezzetta, Inc.
105 Mezzetta Court;
American Canyon, CA 94503;
www.mezzetta.com

Mild to Wild Pepper & Herb Co.
81 Martin Place; Franklin, IN 46131-1745; www.wildpepper.com

Mount Horeb Mustard Museum
Mount Horeb, WI; (800) 438-6878
www.mustardmuseum.com

New Belgium Brewing Company, Fat Tire Ale
Fort Collins, CO
(888) 622-4044
www.newbelgium.com

Quaker Steak and Lube, award-winning wing sauces
Pittsburgh, PA; (412) 494-3344
www.quakersteakandlube.com

Tapatio Hot Sauce
4685 District Boulevard
Vernon, CA 90058-2731
(323) 587-8933
www.Tapatiohotsauce.com

Southern Comfort Creole Barbecue Sauce
Charleston, SC
www.southerncomfort.com

Stone Brewing Company, Arrogant Bastard Ale
155 Mata Way, #104
San Marcos, CA 92069
www.stonebrew.com

Stubb's
P.O. Box 40220; Austin, TX 78704; (512) 480-0203
www.stubbsbbq.com

Whoop Ass Hot Sauce
Southwest Specialty Food, Inc.
700 N. Bullard Avenue
Goodyear, AZ 85338
(800) 536-3131
www.asskickin.com

Index